16021

616.85   Landau, Elaine.
LAN
          Why are they
          starving themselves?

Why Are They STARVING Themselves ?

**Understanding
ANOREXIA NERVOSA and BULIMIA**

Elaine Landau

Introduction by Ellen Schor
Co-director, Associates for Bulimia and
Related Disorders

JULIAN MESSNER
New York

Manufactured in the United States of America

Design by Irving Perkins Associates

10 9 8 7
10 9 8 7 6 5   pbk

Library of Congress Cataloging in Publication Data

Landau, Elaine.
Why are they starving themselves?

Bibliography: p.
Includes index.
Summary: Discusses two eating disorders: anorexia
nervosa, self-induced starvation, and bulimia, the
binge-purge syndrome of overeating.
1. Anorexia nervosa—Juvenile literature.
2. Bulimarexia—Juvenile literature. [1. Anorexia
nervosa. 2. Bulimarexia] I. Title.
RC552.A5L37   1983   616.85′2   82-24913
ISBN 0-671-45582-6
ISBN 0-671-49492-9 Pbk.

For my SKINNY sister
Carol . . .

CONTENTS

INTRODUCTION

In the 80s, eating disorders such as anorexia nervosa and bulimia have become a major concern in the public eye as well as in the professional realm.

Whether or not eating disorders are actually more prevalent today, or whether their emergence from the closet makes it appear so, is not clear. However, we know that the number of victims affected is staggering.

Therefore, the need to educate the mother of the adolescent, the teacher in the schoolroom, the health professional, and young people themselves has become an absolute necessity.

Yet, the anorectic "perfect and fragile little girl" facade and the bulimic "elusive and perfect woman" facade, make them one of the most difficult populations to recognize and treat.

The emotional and physiological damage of those suffering from these eating disorders is as life threatening and as painful as a heroin addiction. I know, because I have suffered and recovered from these "frightening" disorders. I now am a clinical psychologist helping others recover at the Associates for Bulimia and Related Disorders in Manhattan, where I am co-director. I designed the three-day intensive workshop and follow-up program for the treatment of bulimia that is described in the last chapter of this book.

In Elaine Landau's remarkable book, she has given us a comprehensive and compassionate overview of what anorexia and bulimia are all about. Her powerful vignettes are wonderfully true to life, reminding me of so many actual clients that I have treated. Miss Landau gives the reader the crucial facts underlying the personality types, the specific physiological occurrences and most importantly, places to seek help and their differing treatment philosophies.

I find this information invaluable for the general public and have never before seen it as clearly and precisely spelled out. The balance displayed here between the personal anecdotes and the informative discussions make this a well-written and easily readable book. Without sensationalism, Miss Landau gives an accurate and factual picture of how the lives of these people are out of control. She turns an understanding eye to a problem that has only been glimpsed before. In reading this book, the author awakens our senses to the experience of bulimia. One comes away with lasting insights about this addiction.

Miss Landau's sensitive nature has effectively captured the essence of anorexia and it's wicked stepsister, bulimia. It has been a pleasure to know Elaine Landau and to share in her dedication and concern for these special people.

> Ellen Schor
> Co-director, Associates for Bulimia
> and Related Disorders

Why Are They
STARVING
Themselves
?

Chapter
1

MIRROR, MIRROR, ON THE WALL, WHO'S THE THINNEST OF THEM ALL?

Tammy, now a senior at a small surburban high school in New Jersey, won her first beauty contest at the age of fifteen. It was only a small competition sponsored by the businessmen's association of her hometown, but Tammy's picture was in the newspaper, and she did ride on a beautifully decorated float in a small but rather extravagant parade. She received numerous love letters from boys she had never met, two of which even hinted at the prospect of marriage.

Although Tammy came from a fairly comfortable family, she certainly could not be considered rich. She was a sweet, well-liked young girl, but her family had no influential or political connections of any kind. Yet when Tammy announced to her friends and relatives that she was going to enter the beauty contest, everyone felt certain that she would win. For among her many other positive qualities, Tammy possessed one irresistible characteristic—she was extraordinarily beautiful. Just about everyone who met her marveled at her outstanding good looks.

Tammy is fairly tall, about five feet six inches. She has large green eyes and once had a tawny complexion. Her shapely figure was complemented by a long thick mane of naturally blonde hair that hung to her waist. Without really trying, Tammy always seemed to look more like a showgirl than a student.

However, anyone meeting Tammy today for the first time would not believe that she had ever once been capable of winning a beauty contest. She would not be mistaken for an actress or a model, although she could easily pass for a concentration camp victim.

In the past year, Tammy's weight has dropped from one hundred eighteen to eighty-four pounds. She gives the appearance of a skeleton; her arms and legs seem to dangle from her body like wooden sticks. One can easily detect and count her ribs, even from a distance. Tammy's narrow shoulder blades also seem to jut out of her bony frame. Her once smooth peach-colored skin has taken on a yellowish tint over the last few months.

Much of Tammy's full blonde hair has either fallen out or broken off. Whatever strands are left appear brittle and dry and hang from her head in stringy tufts. Perhaps the most dramatic difference in Tammy's appearance, however, is in her face. There's little flesh around her cheeks or chin, and her eyes seem to stare hauntingly out of her head from deeply recessed sockets.

Tammy has been in and out of the hospital three times in the last year. No, she is not suffering from an advanced stage of cancer. Tammy brought on her own physical condition through self-induced starvation. She is a victim of anorexia nervosa.

This disorder, which has been occurring at a rapidly increasing rate in this country over the last ten years, is chiefly characterized by extreme starvation that leads to a catastrophic weight loss. We are not certain of the causes of the disorder, but we do know that anorexia nervosa is becoming more common. Many experts believe that today it poses a serious threat to students in high schools and colleges. Although most physicians once regarded anorexia nervosa as a relatively rare disorder mainly confined to textbooks, today many of these same doctors are faced with human skeletons in their waiting rooms almost on a weekly basis.

What is anorexia nervosa? *Anorexia* means a lack of appetite for food; *nervosa* means having to do with the nerves. Whom does anorexia nervosa afflict? The answer is a very special type of person. Anorexia nervosa victims tend to be young, healthy, attractive girls from fairly affluent and successful families. The typical victim is a girl between thirteen and nineteen who is often considered quite bright and pretty. The disorder does occur occasionally in young boys, but much less often. It rarely affects poor people and is relatively unheard of in the underdeveloped nations.

Anorexia nervosa is a baffling illness. Beautiful, seemingly healthy young women begin to starve themselves—some to the point of death. Often anorectics even claim that they enjoy the sensations of hunger. Many say that feeling hunger pangs affords them the often much needed assurance that they are not gaining weight.

Anorectics are not disgusted by food. On the contrary, their minds are often dominated by thoughts of food; some find it extremely difficult to think of anything else much of the time. What they fear is gaining weight. The most dreaded possibility to an anorectic is that of becoming fat.

The anorectic does not see her body as it actually is. She has no valid concept of the true effect the actual caloric

value of various foods will have on her physical well-
being. Because the genuine effect of food intake is so distorted to the anorectic, she feels forced to control rigidly
whatever she takes into her body.

The anorectic does not allow herself to take any
chances. She can't really feel sure that eating even one
serving of scrambled eggs will not blow her up to a huge
and unattractive size. She can feel comfortable only when
her stomach is completely empty.

Patti, an anorectic for over two years, ate nothing but
two cream-filled cookies a day for more than seven weeks.
She made the first cookie serve as her breakfast and lunch
and she thought of the second cookie as her main meal.

Patti ate the cookies in a ritualistic manner. She cut up
the first cookie into five or six tiny pieces. Patti tried to
stretch eating the cookie throughout the morning. She
called the small morsels her morning snack, and as she ate
the pieces she tried to convince herself that she felt full.
Patti continuously repeated to herself as the hours passed
that she really didn't need anything else.

She ate the second cookie with comparable deliberation. Patti ate it off a dinner plate and even used a linen
napkin. She told her family that she had already eaten out
or at a friend's house. Patti lost close to seventeen pounds
on her self-imposed regime, but she still did not feel secure about her diet.

She expressed a concern that somehow the cookies
might contribute to an unexpected weight gain. To guard
against this anticipated threat, she decided to reduce her
general food intake. Each morning she carefully separated
the two sections of each cookie and with a knife scraped
the cream filling from both. She then proceeded to eat
what remained of the cookies throughout the day in the
same self-prescribed manner. At the time of this writing
Patti is hospitalized; she receives her nourishment in-

travenously in her arm through a plastic tube that dangles from a bottle hung on a tall pole. She is being fed against her will in order to save her life. Before being placed in a hospital, Patti had reduced her food consumption to only one cookie a day, and she had even insisted on scraping the cream filling off that.

Not all anorexia cases are as dramatic as Patti's, but most of these young girls design their own eating rituals to stretch the mental effect of whatever small amount of food they allow themselves. The girls are extremely secretive about the techniques they devise. In the initial stages of the disorder, many can continue to dine with their families, without their parents' becoming aware that any problem exists.

Melissa, a thirteen-year-old anorectic, began, for instance, simply by selecting one instead of two lamb chops from the meat platter at the family dinner table. To make the lamb chop last for the duration of the meal, Melissa cut the chop into very tiny pieces. Before she allowed herself to swallow even a morsel, she chewed each bite seventy times; she counted silently as she moved her jaws. She also drank large amounts of water between bites to give herself a feeling of fullness.

Melissa applied the same procedures to the other foods served. She would choose only one vegetable and take a very small portion of it. She would then cut it into very small pieces and chew and swallow it with slow deliberation. In this manner she was able to finish her dinner at about the same time the other members of the family did, while only eating about one-third as much food. It wasn't until she had undergone a noticeable weight loss that her parents realized how little she actually ate.

Karen, a sixteen-year-old anorectic, starved herself while enjoying vicarious pleasure watching others eat. After Karen's illness had progressed somewhat, she insisted on becoming the family chef. Although it seemed to them a very contradictory request, Karen's parents consented to their daughter's desire because they thought that any interest in food at all might mean a step toward recovery. Unfortunately, it did not.

Karen pretended she was eating as she watched others enjoy food. Others did the chewing, swallowing, and weight gaining for her. Much of her desire for food became immersed in the elaborate dishes she created for her family and friends. She rose earlier than the rest of her family in order to prepare special blueberry pancakes or ice cream waffles for their breakfast. She made blueberry muffins and chocolate chip cookies for her little brother to take in his school lunch box.

Karen dug up elaborate pizza recipes to make special snacks for her friends. Although prior to the onset of her illness Karen had been an excellent student, she now spent her after-school hours creating tasty French cuisine for her family's dinner instead of studying.

After a few weeks, Karen's older sister simply refused to eat any more of Karen's magnificent meals. She found that she had put on weight and was having difficulty fitting into several of her favorite outfits. In the past, Karen's mother had usually prepared simple evening meals that generally consisted of lean meats and vegetables.

Karen's sister said she couldn't understand why everyone was now forced to eat a different rich French sauce each night, especially since Karen never even took a bite of her own cooking. The discussion led to a great deal of conflict and a number of angry outbursts within the family. Things were resolved only when Karen's sister received permission to cook her own less lavish evening meals alongside her sister in the kitchen.

Another unpleasant incident involving Karen's obsession with food occurred one Saturday afternoon while she was baby-sitting for her neighbor's son. The little boy was six, and Karen had been taking care of him since he was almost four. The two had a good relationship, and when Karen watched him on Saturday afternoons, she always allowed him to invite several young friends over for company.

On this particular Saturday, Karen had prepared a special treat for the children: she made each a large ice cream sundae overflowing with hot fudge sauce. The children were delighted, except for one little girl who had had ice cream earlier in the day, did not feel hungry now, and did not want to finish the sundae Karen had prepared. For no apparent reason, Karen lashed out at the little girl. She raised her voice, called the child ungrateful, and snatched the dish away from the child hurriedly. The young girl ran home in tears. Karen later confessed that she felt terrible about what had happened and simply did not understand what had caused her to become so overly incensed.

The preoccupation of an anorectic with feeding others and thereby feeding herself vicariously can take many forms. One girl who had lost over fifty pounds insisted on baking more than four dozen brownies for her school's bake sale. Another got a weekend job in a candy store until she became too emaciated to continue working or going to school. These activities become incorporated into each girl's way of dealing with her illness and the method she has chosen by which to starve herself systematically.

At the height of her illness an anorectic may come to look and feel like a hideous nightmare. Her skin will become dry; her hair will break off; she may suffer from anemia. Many anorectics stop menstruating, and often when their weight drops sufficiently low, a layer of soft hair begins to grow on their backs. It's almost as if these very skinny individuals are beginning to become covered with a layer of down.

The anorectic does not see herself as she really is, however. She never has, and that is part of the reason she may have become ill initially. The anorectic believes that she looks her best when she is at her lowest possible weight. Even when forced to look at themselves in a mirror wearing only a bikini, emaciated anorectics will often claim that they look disgustingly fat. One skeletonlike young woman who had lost almost sixty pounds in a year protested bitterly that her stomach still stuck out and that her thighs looked too fat and flabby.

Feeling hunger makes the anorectic feel thin, and feeling thin permits the anorectic to feel she is in control of her body and therefore somewhat in control of her life. This is very important to the type of girl who becomes an anorexia nervosa victim, as previously she might have felt like little more than a puppet manipulated by other people in her life.

As Stella, a seventeen-year-old anorectic, expressed it, "When I was able to lose weight and keep it off, I finally felt as though I was in charge of my own welfare. It was strange, but wonderful—a sort of powerful feeling. I felt as though now I was allowed to please myself. I had my own expectations of how thin I wanted to be, and I pursued my own goal.

"Before, when I was heavier, I had always obeyed. I did everything anyone in charge told me to do. Somehow being thin—I mean having the willpower to become very slender and stay thin—made me feel superior to people who have a ring of flab around their middle. I felt strong and powerful for the first time in my life. I was exhilarated by the whole experience. Whenever I felt as though my mother or teachers were about to overpower me, I'd silently vow to lose still another pound. It always seemed to make me feel as though I had won."

The anorectic takes tremendous pride in her emaciation. She doesn't regard herself as excessively thin but as on the road to a trimmer figure. An anorectic never feels she's thin enough. She may be quick to point out to her critics that all successful models and many actresses are actually underweight. To the anorectic, achieving ultra-thinness means capturing both beauty and control. The anorectic is extremely proud of both her slender frame and the willpower she had to generate to achieve it.

Jenny, a sixteen-year-old anorectic, had always been a very pleasant and popular girl before she became ill. When her friends and family pleaded with her to stop starving herself once the symptoms of her anorexia had surfaced, however, she grew to distrust them. Jenny became sullen and distant and seemed to withdraw into herself a great deal of the time. She later described her feelings this way: "I felt just awful. It was as though everyone I had ever cared about at all had turned on me. I guess I never had any real friends at all.

"I finally looked thin. Not as slender as I wanted to become, but I felt as though I was going to get there. It turned out that everyone I knew became terribly jealous of me. They were hurt because I was able to do something they weren't. My friends are always going on diets, but they are rarely successful. Even when they did lose a few pounds, they seemed to put it all right back on. They were still fat. They were bulging out in every direction, and they simply couldn't stand the fact that I looked better than they did.

"Most of my clothes became too big for me to wear. Even my favorite outfits were swimming on me. My mother bought me a few new pieces, but when they also became too large to wear comfortably, she flatly refused to purchase another item for me. She said I was ungrateful, foolish, and stupid for destroying my own good looks.

"But what I can't understand is why my mother refused

to admit that I looked better now than ever before in my life. A mother may wish for a cute, plump baby, but a pudgy teenager is an entirely different story.

"The situation with my sister and friends was even more tragic. All they seemed to talk about now was how I was destroying myself, and how could I go on doing this. Even though I had demonstrated tremendous willpower, shown strength that they could probably never muster up, no one ever even hinted at what I had actually accomplished. I never got any praise for doing what they couldn't do. The thinner I became, the more everyone seemed to drift away from me. My friends just couldn't see how special I was. They began to treat me as though I were weird.

"My sister—she's only a year and a half younger than I am—decided to take advantage of the whole situation. At first she begged me to eat. I guess she felt it was her duty to encourage me to gain weight. But after a while she seemed interested only in inheriting the clothes that were too big for me. She really seemed thrilled when my mother handed over the new outfits to her.

"We had always been such good friends, but now our friendship seemed to distintegrate slowly. My sister seemed bored with my condition. She accused me of not eating just to get attention. I felt upset by the loss of our closeness, but I just let our friendship slip away."

The anorectic's greatest achievement is her slenderness. She firmly believes that what she has done is a unique accomplishment, and she is usually willing to do just about anything to retain the special status she feels her condition bestows on her.

Mirror, Mirror, on the wall,
Who's the thinnest of them all?

Each anorectic hopes it is she.

THE GOOD LITTLE LADY

Sugar and spice and everything nice . . . that's what anorectics are made of. . . .

Many anorectics come from "perfect" homes; they seemingly enjoy the type of enviable family life most people read about in magazines but never experience. The anorectic usually develops in an upper middle-class environment in which there is ample affluence to satisfy her material needs as well as those of the other family members. She usually is well dressed, goes to the best schools, and at an early age has been introduced to and begun to participate in numerous cultural activities of one sort or another.

Anorectics may be free of the burdens put on young people who come from less advantaged homes, but to some this very freedom becomes a burden in itself. Because their parents give them so much, anorectics often feel that they must live up to unrealistically high expectations to please other family members, teachers, and friends.

The anorectic is always frightened about not doing well enough and is almost haunted by an irrational fear of failure. She may constantly compare herself with others around her, but she never feels superior. Even the small successes of others serve only to underscore her inadequacy.

At only sixteen years of age, Maggie had graduated from high school and been accepted at an Ivy League college. She was thrilled by the idea of attending college, but at the same time she felt overly terrified at the possible prospect of not doing well. Unfortunately, once she arrived at the university, Maggie allowed her fear of failure to prevent her from achieving even as much as she was capable of. She spent so much of her time memorizing small details, to make sure she did not miss anything, that she often failed to digest fully or comprehend the meaning of important concepts inherent in the materials that she studied.

She was especially afraid of not doing well in calculus, as math had never been her strong subject. She sorely neglected the subjects she usually did well in so she could devote more time to math. Because this was an extremely difficult subject for which Maggie had little talent, however, she found that she still did not score as highly as she had hoped to, and now her other subjects suffered as well.

Her report card for the first marking period contained four B's and two C's. Maggie, who had always previously maintained an A average, felt horrified. Instead of seeing the situation realistically and adjusting her study habits to help remedy her predicament, however, Maggie panicked. She confided to her roommate that she felt frightened and as though she had "lost control over her life."

A few days after the grade reports were given out, Maggie began a strenuous diet. She told her friends that if she did not spend so much time worrying about her weight, she would probably do better academically. By the end of the new term, Maggie had lost seventy-six pounds. After various forms of therapy had failed, Maggie was taken from her dormitory and placed in a hospital where she was fed intravenously. She remained hospitalized until she began to gain some weight.

The anorectic feels that she must do well in life to repay her family for all the advantages they have showered on her. She will frequently resort to inordinate means not to offend or disappoint her parents in even the smallest way.

Carla, a seventeen-year-old anorectic, had been given permission to redecorate her own room. She was allowed a generous budget and was told she could purchase whatever she desired within the allotted amount.

Carla was genuinely excited at the prospect of redoing her room by herself. She bought several decorating magazines and checked out from her local library a book on interior design. She spoke to different neighbors whose homes showed a taste she admired, and she tried out her own ideas on several of her girl friends. Carla felt that this was a very important undertaking, and she wanted to act responsibly in making her decisions.

After a few weeks of intensive research, Carla was finally able to envision her dream room. It was all to be done in the style of India. She would drape the walls with fabric, purchase an imitation Oriental rug as well as a bamboo headboard and chest of drawers. She had planned to spend the weekend upstate visiting her older sister at college, and she was so proud of her plans that she even drew some sketches of the room to show to her sister.

When Carla returned home from her sister's campus that Sunday night, however, the sight that greeted her filled her with pain. She returned to her room to find that it had already been redecorated by someone else. There was a deep pink rug, a white canopy bed, and a floral ruffled bedspread. It was nothing like the new room Carla had planned, and she took an almost immediate dislike to every new item in it.

About thirty seconds after she'd switched on the bedroom light, Carla heard her mother squeal the word, *"Surprise!"* Her mother gave Carla a big hug and then joyously went on to explain how she just knew that Carla would love the room, since the two of them were so much alike. She continued, going on to express how much Carla had always liked the clothes she chose for her, as well as how Carla had enjoyed the toys her mother had brought home for her when Carla was younger.

Carla felt as though she'd been demolished. All her plans for a room that was truly her own had disintegrated. She wondered why her parents had offered her an individual choice and money to spend if it was all to be withdrawn at her mother's whim. Carla felt as if her own feelings didn't really count. It was almost as if she were a nonperson.

Carla, however, tried very hard to dismiss her pain and disappointment. She forced herself to swallow her anger. Her foremost concern was not to hurt her mother's feelings. Carla was determined that her mother not be made to feel any anguish over this incident, and so she promised herself never to let anyone know what her true feelings were.

Carla simply returned her mother's embrace and praised her parents' good taste. She even thanked her mother for being so thoughtful as to have saved her the time it would take to come up with a decorating scheme of her own.

Carla's mother left the room feeling that she had done a wonderful job. She was proud of herself and felt certain that she was an outstanding parent. She had no idea that Carla secretly wished she could tear up the rug. Carla managed to squelch any negative feelings she had about the new decor, and she never again spoke to anyone about her plans to pick out her own stylish bamboo headboard.

Unfortunately, Carla's entire life was dominated by many incidents similar to the one described here. In an overzealous effort to please her parents and become the child of their dreams in every way, Carla consistently stifled her own growth and development as a healthy individual. She somehow lost track of her own needs and desires. Carla became an overly submissive child at the cost of her own identity.

The onset of Carla's anorexia might have been her own way of striking back. She had already given up the freedom of making her own choices. Her body weight may have appeared to her the only thing left that she felt she could control. It seemed to be the only area in which she allowed herself to assert any form of power at all.

A number of common characteristics are associated with the type of home from which most anorectics come. The families tend to be small; often there are only one or two children. The parents of anorectic children are often older than the average parent at the time of the child's birth. In many cases the mother was in her thirties or early forties when the child was delivered.

There is often a scarcity of boys in the homes of young anorectic women. Statistics show that most anorectics do not have brothers. In instances where there is a boy in the family, he is often the youngest child, and his anorectic sister is generally a number of years older.

In families in which there are no sons, the fathers of anorectic girls may tend to place unrealistic expectations on their daughters. Some of these young female children become responsible at a very young age for "carrying on the family name." They are expected to shine both in athletics and in academic work. A father may view such a girl as primarily an extension of himself, and he may expect her to perform brilliantly in all areas of her life. In a number of instances, anorectic girls remembered that their fathers had chided them for putting on even a few pounds prior to the onset of their illness.

Studies of the mothers of anorectics reveal that these women often appear to be quite secure and self-assured on the surface. They are conscientious parents, perhaps overly so in some cases, who are genuinely concerned with rearing their children correctly. These mothers often speak with tremendous pride when describing the "ideal" child they helped to mold before the girl became anorectic. They are usually shocked by the sudden appearance of anorexia and express their disbelief that a sweet and obedient girl such as their daughter could turn into such a stubborn and willfully determined noneater.

Although she may not always be conscious of it, the anorectic's mother often wants to be a "supermom" who is interested in producing a superior child. Such a mother becomes overly involved with her child, pouring all her time, energy, and devotion into this little person. In return for her very costly and personal investment, the child must please her, become the embodiment of what she considers desirable. The child must give up her own autonomy. The young girl is strongly discouraged from growing up to be a separate individual with the broad range of feelings and emotions common to all human beings. Instead, she must become a model of perfection, reflecting only those qualities that her parents deem desirable.

Studies have also shown that the anorectic's mother is frequently a professional woman who has given up her career at least for a time in order to devote herself more freely to her family. Often these women are quite concerned with appearance and place a great deal of emphasis on making themselves appear as physically attractive as possible. Some may even seem obsessed with the desire that others regard them as exceptionally pretty.

Kathy Wilder, a fourteen-year-old anorectic, described her mother as looking more like a movie star than a housewife. She noted that several of her friends from school and even her algebra teacher had commented on how much her mother resembled the actress Farrah Fawcett.

Indeed, Mrs. Wilder was considered a very attractive woman. It always made Kathy giggle when teenage boys whistled at her mother or when her mother made heads turn at the beach. She was proud of her mother's good looks, but even though the two were very close, Kathy remained somewhat in awe of her mother.

To some degree, however, the whole family paid a price for the mother's good looks. Mrs. Wilder made a point of reading all the latest fashion magazines, and she insisted on dressing in style. Kathy and her sister frequently heard arguments between her mother and father over the amount of money her mother spent on clothes and makeup. After she became ill, Kathy vividly recalled a heated argument over what her mother spent on a new fur jacket. Her father angrily stormed out of the house and did not return until the next day.

The incident involving her mother's appearance that Kathy remembers most vividly took place when Kathy was ten years old. Her parents had planned a large and extravagant party to celebrate New Year's Eve. They had invited a number of her father's most important clients, and Kathy remembers that they spared no expense. They purchased several pieces of furniture, hired a fine caterer and staff, and brought in a string quartet to play chamber music. Kathy remembered that by early evening the entire house was decked out in flowers and that each room smelled like a bouquet.

Her mother had purchased a magnificent full-length white silk evening gown for the occasion, and although Kathy and her sister were expected to retire well before midnight, their mother bought each of her daughters a beautiful new bright blue taffeta party dress.

Everyone felt excited about the affair, but when Mrs. Wilder returned from the hairdresser the afternoon of the party, all their plans fell into shambles. In an effort to look her best for the evening, Kathy's mother had had her hair not only washed and set as usual but restyled as well.

Kathy thought her mother looked more beautiful than ever, but Mrs. Wilder was furious with the beautician. She claimed that he had restyled her hair badly and had cut it too short. She claimed that the hairdo made her face look too full and her neck too long.

Upon returning home from the beauty parlor, Kathy's mother was filled with rage. There seemed to be nothing that anyone could do to calm her. She screamed at Kathy and slapped Kathy's younger sister across the face with little provocation. Then Mrs. Wilder went to her own room, flung herself down on the bed, and cried hysterically for over an hour and a half.

When her sobs finally diminished, she confronted herself in the mirror, claimed that her eyes were now badly swollen, and began to cry all over again at the sight of herself. Mrs. Wilder kept repeating that she looked and felt horrible. She was clearly out of control.

It was frightening for Kathy and her sister to watch their mother having a temper tantrum. Mrs. Wilder's outburst continued. No one seemed able to calm her or make her listen to reason. She informed her husband that she would not leave their bedroom, and under no circumstances would she attend the party that evening. She said that she refused to be seen looking like a witch.

For the first time, Kathy realized the depth of her mother's vanity. In actuality, her mother looked quite good, but Mrs. Wilder did not think so, and on the basis of that assumption she was willing to ruin everyone's evening.

Unfortunately, Kathy's mother remained true to her word. She did not leave her room all evening. Her husband found himself in an awkward predicament. It was very difficult for Mr. Wilder, by himself, to see that everything ran smoothly. He was forced to entertain his numerous guests alone. Mr. Wilder tried to make an excuse for his wife's absence, but he doubted whether anyone believed him.

The incident was not discussed after that evening, but Kathy still remembers that New Year's Eve with vivid clarity. And the Wilders never gave another party.

Susan, age sixteen, is another anorectic daughter of a very attractive but vain woman. It seems that, in her late teens, Susan's mother had attracted the attention of a number of young men at her university with her beautiful smile and her attractive figure. Over the years she went to great lengths never to let anyone forget this fact.

Now at forty-seven, she still wished to be appreciated for the same qualities. She was determined to keep her weight down, and although she usually cooked sumptuous meals for the rest of her family, she prepared for herself only a small salad, which she ate with little or no dressing.

She often boasted that although her teenage daughter Susan wore a size nine, she had managed to maintain her own size seven figure throughout the years. Susan's mother exercised at home, belonged to a spa, and spent a good deal of time in front of the mirror. She never purchased any article of clothing unless she believed that it made her look slender. Unfortunately, she demanded comparably high standards from her daughter.

Frequently the parents of anorectic children will speak at length about the superior home environment they've provided for their child. One mother, who had formerly been a children's librarian but had given up her job to raise a family, stressed that by the time her daughter was two, she had personally selected over one hundred picture books for the little girl's own library.

Often the parents of anorectic children have gone to great lengths to provide their offspring with special advantages. Many of these now very slender girls have been given art, music, dancing, and tennis lessons. They have been taken to museums, libraries, and other cultural centers almost from the time they learned to walk.

These parents provide generous glowing descriptions of a fulfilling and harmonious home life. Most treasure countless memories of how their daughter won a tennis trophy, was the youngest student to star in the spelling bee, or was the best dancer in her class recital. When faced with the reality of having a child who is suffering from anorexia nervosa, they will often initially deal with it by continuously recounting what they view as the joyous moments of their family's past.

Ironically, at the onset of their illness, anorexia victims often claim that they are as pleased with their home life as their parents are. Many girls sound as if the illness were their only problem rather than an outward symptom of very deep underlying conflicts.

Anorexia victims are sometimes afraid to admit to anyone, even to themselves, that they feel troubled. They are supposed to be perfect little girls living in perfect little worlds. Some believe that admitting there may be a problem or voicing even the slightest criticism of their home life would constitute a betrayal of their parents. These girls believe they should be grateful for all their families have given them. If they experience unsettling feelings, they are not quite sure how to deal with them.

Unfortunately, all the advantages offered by the typical anorectic's family place a difficult burden on the young person. Before the onset of her illness, the anorectic may have been continuously under a strain. In some instances, she may not have fully realized just how much pressure she was actually being made to deal with. All her activities are often motivated by the need to prove that her mother and father are both superior parents and people as demonstrated through her own outstanding performance. The anorectic child is expected to return a great deal for the social and financial benefits provided by her parents.

A portion of the anorectic's unconscious payback to her parents is the display of perfect manners and behavior prior to her illness. These little girls are exceedingly polite to everyone at all times. The anorectic never allows herself to misbehave or to act like a spoiled child.

She makes a point of never expressing negative feelings of any variety, and she learns early in life that to win her parents' praise she must swallow her anger. This type of girl is very much concerned with what people will think of her; the impression she makes on others is usually foremost in her mind.

Anorectics are generally superior students. Both the girls and their parents take pride in the child's academic performance. Although anorectic young women tend to be intelligent, they are not necessarily brilliant or gifted. Often their success is the result of continuous diligent effort.

Although Lisa, a fourteen-year-old anorectic, had never

experienced any real difficulty in successfully completing her school assignments, the semester before she was about to enter high school, like many anorectics, she panicked at the prospect of not achieving the same high grades she had earned in junior high. As the months passed, Lisa's anxiety intensified, and by summer Lisa confided to her parents that she was terrified of having her grade average fall when she started high school.

Instead of comforting Lisa and assuring her that if she studied she'd do well, Lisa's parents became as anxious as their own young daughter. They overreacted to the situation. Her mother and father visited the new high school, found out what courses Lisa would be taking in the fall and what texts would be used in her classes.

Lisa's parents then went to the expense of purchasing all the textbooks required. That summer Lisa was outfitted with a full supply of books, pens, paper, and notebooks. Each morning the parents arranged for Lisa to work privately with a tutor who came to their home.

Without meaning to, Lisa's parents had actually increased the pressures their daughter was suffering under. With all the money, time, and attention being lavished on her that summer, Lisa felt more obligated than ever to do well. To make sure she'd be able to hold up her end of the bargain, Lisa studied all summer more diligently than ever before. Her parents had also purchased an individual membership in a swim club for her that summer, but Lisa hardly ever went. The few times she allowed herself to go she felt guilty that she was enjoying herself when perhaps she should be studying. Lisa became a driven child. She believed she would do just about anything to avoid even the slightest criticism from her teachers or parents once the new term began.

Her formerly conscientious attitude had gotten out of hand. Ironically, at the close of the new fall term, Lisa's grades were about the same as they had been in the past. And if only for just a moment, Lisa allowed herself to believe that her average might have been about the same even if she hadn't put herself through the rigors of the past summer.

The anorectic's view of herself and her approach to life affect her friendships as well as her home and school life. Often this type of girl proves to be overly compliant in her relationships with others. She is so eager to be accepted and well liked that she remains submissive in the face of the demands of others.

The anorectic is determined to be a people-pleaser at almost any cost to herself. Often she will have one very close friend, and she may devote a good deal of effort to trying to become very much like this friend. Greta, a thirteen-year-old anorectic, described her feelings this way: "Last year Sarah was my best friend. I had always admired her, she was quite popular in school, and everyone who met her seemed to like her. I was thrilled that she let me be her friend, but I always somehow felt afraid around her. I mean, what if I said something that made her angry and she dropped me? I'd be so embarrassed, and I think I'd probably be alone. I've always had to work very hard to have friends. People just never run after me the way they pursue Sarah.

"It's hard for me to meet new people. It's not that I'm shy. Oh, definitely not. My parents have always stressed what a deficiency it is to be bashful. They tell people that none of their children has ever been shy. We're all brave Johnson kids willing to tackle anything.

"Still, I usually feel awkward going to a place if I don't already know most of the people there. Last summer Sarah invited me to spend a weekend with her at her aunt's beach house. I thought it would be fun because her aunt's house is right on the ocean, and I love to swim.

"I did have a good time until Sarah's aunt suggested that we go to a dance for young people in a neighboring town on Saturday night. The whole idea of going to a strange dance in a strange place terrified me, but Sarah seemed thrilled at the prospect of it and jumped at the opportunity to go.

"Her aunt offered to drive us to the dance, but I said I'd rather walk and enjoy the view along the beach. Sarah and her aunt believed me, but actually I was just buying time. I thought my trip would take about half an hour longer than the drive, and it would mean that much less time that I'd be forced to be at the dance.

"When I finally arrived at the dance, it took me about forty-five minutes to get myself through the door. I felt a huge lump in my throat, and I had difficulty swallowing, but I knew I had to go through with this. Even though I honestly did not want to be at this dance, I was afraid to go home because I thought that Sarah might be angry at me.

"Yet Sarah hardly paid attention to me for the rest of the evening. She danced with several boys and spent over an hour talking to two new girls she met there while she was waiting for me to arrive. One guy asked me to dance. He looked okay, but I said no. I guess I didn't feel like it. I felt very lonely standing there for most of the evening by myself. It was very hard to get Sarah's attention; she just seemed so busy. Maybe I didn't have to go to that dance after all. I still really don't know. I was just so afraid of ruining Sarah's vacation weekend. After all, she was my best friend."

Margot, a cured twenty-year-old former anorectic, described her similar relationships with her friends before she became ill: "I was just like a blank slate around other people. I'd be whatever I thought they wanted me to be. I always tried to say whatever I believed they wished to hear. I was never my own person. I never expressed any thoughts, feelings, or original ideas.

"But after all, how could I when in reality I didn't have anything to say that was uniquely my own? My parents had just never seen it as their obligation to mold me into a separate individual. I was just supposed to be a darling little girl. Perfect behavior and unquestioning obedience. I became just what I was expected to be and nothing more. Then I got very ill. I guess something had to happen eventually. You just can't crush a human being like that to fit a mold that was somebody else's conception to begin with."

Some anorectic girls may be exceedingly popular. This does not necessarily indicate that these young women are especially likable; rather quite often they just put far more effort into winning and maintaining friendships than the average young person does.

If the anorectic girl even suspects that it is important to her parents that she have a large social circle, she will try to do so. To ensure that they will not be disliked, these girls may flatter, buy small presents, give up their turn, or continually go out of their way to do something extra for someone. They will try to please almost to the point of servitude.

Even though the anorectic continuously reflects meticulous behavior, she frequently evaluates herself as overloaded with shortcomings. She finds it increasingly difficult to live up to the extraordinarily high standards she has set for herself. Eventually she must confront the fact that it is virtually impossible always to please everyone.

Chapter
3

FLYING HIGH LIKE AN EAGLE — WHAT IT FEELS LIKE TO STARVE

"I feel like an exquisite bird today. Not like a turquoise peacock strutting around with its tail out in an open fan. Those birds are beautiful though. I feel more like an eagle flying high in the air, above the soaring mountains. It's as if now I'm invincible. I'm not afraid of anyone, and nothing can touch me. I'm a strong, fearless bird with my own power, and it's coming from deep inside me.

"Today I feel as if I could probably get a modeling job. Even though I've never worked as a model before, I think I might finally be thin enough. This has been the best day yet for me. I feel stronger today. Whenever I don't eat—when I'm finally able to stand it and I don't give in to the hunger—I feel strangely superior. I believe that if I can do this, I can do anything."

These words are a direct quotation from Patti, a fifteen-year-old anorectic who resided in Queens, New York. They only reflect one phase of Patti's feelings, however. While she was at the same weight at which she described herself as being strong as a soaring eagle, she often referred to herself as a fat, ugly watermelon. At one point, Patti told her therapist that if the watermelon took one more bite, it would probably burst.

Although Patti worked with a private therapist on a daily basis, she continued her regime of starvation. She was admitted to a hospital several times. Once hospitalized, she was fed intravenously. Her circulation was poor and her electrolyte level affected. (The electrolyte level is the balance of chemicals in the body essential for health.) Yet whenever Patti began to gain weight or even to maintain her present weight level, she claimed that she hated herself, that her body disgusted her.

On several different occasions in the hospital, she ripped the IV tube out of her arm. Finally she left the hospital against medical orders. Patti ran away, and her parents were unable to locate her. They later learned that she stayed in the apartment of an older friend who had dropped out of college.

Patti never grew up to become a soaring eagle in any respect. She never came to feel genuinely competent and secure as an adult. Six months after she fled from the hospital for the last time, Patti's body rested on a slab in the morgue. She never lived to become the model she thought she could be or to become anything else, for that matter. She proved to be one of the unlucky ones. In a macabre way, however, Patti had been successful. She had succeeded in starving herself to death.

Time after time in the midst of their illness, anorectics will express the feeling that not eating affords them a supreme sense of superiority. Being thin makes them feel important and worthwhile if only for a short time. It's as though the young woman experiences a temporary and extremely distorted sense of competence.

The anorectic is the champion of self-denial. She pours most of her energy into denying that she needs any food and into overcoming the constant demands of hunger. Some anorectics divide their day into one-hour segments, hoping that if they can make it through the last minutes of the hour without taking a bite of food, then they'll be that much closer to their goal. Completing the day having adhered to their own rigid diet allowance gives the anorectic a personal sense of victory. The anorectic tries to solve all her problems and anxieties by manipulating her body size through starvation.

Some therapists believe that the anorectic's unconscious desire not to grow up but to remain a little girl is a factor in her illness. Many of these girls seem shocked and alarmed over the bodily changes that normally occur during puberty. Often they become determined to be ultraslim as soon as their breasts begin to develop and their bodies soften into curves.

Joan, a fourteen-year-old anorectic who had excelled in athletics from her early youth, had always been considered something of a tomboy. Her father had been her coach as well as her most ardent athletic promoter, and when she was nine, Joan was one of the first girls to play on a little league team. She was also an excellent skier and swimmer.

Joan often played softball with her two older brothers who took tremendous pride in offering their little sister helpful tips to develop her skill.

For several years Joan was a regular player in a weekend softball game with a number of boys her own age who lived in her neighborhood. As time passed, however, and as Joan's body began to develop, she found that the boys no longer regarded her as simply another player. Once she heard some of them making joking remarks about her breasts, and another boy asked her to see a movie with him.

Joan did not feel flattered by this new attention from

boys. In fact, the whole concept of even a casual relationship with a member of the opposite sex seemed to terrify
her. Joan felt afraid of the social demands that would be
placed on her as a teenager. She began an exceptionally
stringent diet, which she kept up for over two years. Joan
hoped to starve off her breasts and the curves of her hips
in an effort to avoid the responsibilities of womanhood.
By trying to make her body straight and flat like that of a
young girl, Joan hoped to recapture the asexual security of
childhood.

The threat of approaching puberty signals distress to
many of these girls. Often they are upset by the reality of
menstruation and feel unusually uncomfortable with the
monthly flow of blood every normal woman must contend
with. As the anorectic's weight drops, her monthly period
will usually stop. In some ways this is extremely comforting to these girls because it enables them to feel less like
adult women.

Although anorectics are often reluctant to admit it,
many secretly wish that they had been born males rather
than females. Some will speak at great length of being
envious of the opportunities offered to boys for independence and assertive behavior. Without fully realizing
it, the anorectic may want her extremely slender body to
be more like a man's body and therefore capable in some
unrealistic way of granting her the same freedom and authority she attributes to being male.

Often the onset of anorexia nervosa follows a traumatic
incident in a young girl's life. In many instances this
casual factor involves a meaningful loss or follows a
dramatic change in the anorectic's environment. The
young person may feel unable to cope with the situation
or to handle the experience with ease or security.

Attending a new high school or college, moving to a
new neighborhood, entering any new highly competitive

endeavor, and being the only child remaining in the home after an older brother or sister has left have all been identified as triggers that have set off the illness in numerous cases.

Faith, for instance, was a finalist in a college writing competition that won her a summer internship at a major New York publishing house. At first Faith appeared delighted with her success, but as the weeks passed and her trip to New York approached, she felt intimidated and frightened by the challenge.

Faith had never been away from home without her parents for any length of time, and although she would be staying in a hotel accompanied by a chaperon and the eleven other finalists, she was afraid that she would be lonely.

She also lacked confidence in her writing ability. Faith had spent a number of hours on her winning essay but still never believed that the piece had any genuine literary merit. She worried that she would not be able to satisfy the publisher's expectations, and she was also afraid that her work would not match the standards set by the other girls. In the three months before she was to leave for New York, Faith lost almost forty pounds. She continued to lose weight, and eventually her New York trip was canceled.

In some cases, an extremely hurtful remark or incident regarding diet or weight control serves as the surface causal factor. For example, Judy, a fifteen-year-old anorectic, was shopping with her mother for a new pair of jeans when her mother remarked that Judy's stomach was really beginning to stick out unattractively. Her mother went on to say that whenever her daughter put on a few pounds, it seemed to go to the same spot. She suggested that they purchase one or two overblouses for Judy.

In response Judy sucked in her stomach and took a long

hard look at herself in the mirror. At that moment her stomach appeared enormous to her. She decided that she didn't like the jeans she had on or any of the other pairs she tried on subsequently. Judy left the store without making any purchases. That evening she began a strict diet that eventually turned into anorexia nervosa.

When Megan was fifteen, she went to a church-sponsored Saturday night dance with two of her girl friends. Although both girl friends were asked to dance at least once during the evening, Megan was not. Megan stood near a very attractive boy at the dance, but her hopes were shattered when she overheard him tell the boy standing next to him that he thought she was cute but a little chunky. Although Megan didn't even know this boy, she regarded his opinion as unquestionable. Megan was not overweight, but she became determined to shed some pounds. Within six months she had lost sixty pounds and was diagnosed as anorectic.

Although such negative events or experiences as these may appear to set off the illness, there are always deeper underlying problems that make a person become a victim of anorexia nervosa.

Chapter
4

IN HER OWN WORDS

Laurie is a seventeen-year-old anorectic from Westchester County, New York. In a group psychotherapy session, she related how she felt when her illness began. What she said was tape-recorded and later typed into a transcript. These are Laurie's actual words:

"I remember that I first started to feel badly the day I saw a sign advertising a dance at school. The dance was 'Cupid's Follies,' an annual girl-ask-boy Valentine's Day dance. I know that I wanted to go. I mean, I always wanted to go, but I had never attended yet during the three years I had been in high school, and I somehow felt I wouldn't be attending this year either.

"When I came home from school that day and tried to do my homework, I just felt so dissatisfied. Nothing in my life was the way I wanted it to have been. I knew that lately I had been feeling angry a good deal of the time. Still, I wasn't exactly sure what or who I was angry at.

"I pushed aside my notebook and stood in front of the full-length mirror in my room. I stood there for what

33

seemed like an eternity, smiling, making faces at myself, piling my hair on top of my head, and then letting it fall back to my shoulders.

"The next moment I peeled off my clothes. Baring myself in front of the mirror with nothing on but my bra and panties, I felt mortified. My body seemed like a map replete with mountains of flesh and fat. I wore only a size nine, but looking at myself in the mirror I thought I looked more like a size 18½, perhaps a full size 24½.

"I couldn't stand it. I hated the way I looked. I went to the closet and pulled out my favorite dress. It was a red silk with a Chinese collar. I always thought it was especially flattering to me, but tonight it seemed to make me look like a miniature Buddha. I took off my beloved red dress, threw it on the floor, and returned to my closet for something else.

"This time I pulled out my turquoise turtleneck sweater and blue velvet designer jeans. I tried them on and looked at myself. I wanted to smash the mirror. I had purchased the tight jeans to try to look glamorous, but now the tight-waisted jeans only seemed to make my abdomen bulge. An instant later, my blue outfit joined my red silk dress on the floor.

"I proceeded to try on my charcoal gray tunic when I heard a rap at the door. I knew that knock, and I also knew it meant that in less than an instant my mother would come prancing into the room. And worst of all, I knew there was nothing I could do about it.

"My mother looked around at the mess in my room. She sarcastically asked me if I was putting on a fashion show or doing an early spring cleaning. She left to make dinner, saying that she thought a smart girl like me would have something better to do than play tornado in my room.

"I picked up the blue sweater and jeans off the floor. I clutched the soft velvet against my belly and felt guilty for so casually discarding them on the floor. They were a gift from my dad. My mother had always thought that the outfit looked too sexy and had discouraged me from wearing it, but dad and I had chosen it together.

"I remember thinking then that I had had a wonderful day and had bought a wonderful outfit, but somehow the experience was losing its magic. Lately my father barely had time to talk to me. It was almost as if he were purposely ignoring me. And now I felt that the outfit made me look fat.

"My mother called me to come downstairs and help her make dinner. I went, but I realized that in the last few months, I had begun to feel a sense of unease when I was around my mother. It was as if in my mother's presence I was like a marionette with my mom pulling all the strings.

"Even when I was very little I remember always feeling overwhelmed by my mother. Mother has a strong and often overpowering personality. My father always compares her to a heavy perfume that dominates the air. But mom really doesn't look the type. Physically, my mother is a short, slight, naturally blonde woman, who at the age of forty-two has managed to keep her size six figure. Men still find mom attractive, and I think it's obvious to most people who meet my mother that she also believes herself to be a very good-looking woman.

"When I arrived in the kitchen, I was greeted by the sight of my mother and my younger sister Minnie, cutting the ingredients for this evening's salad. Standing together side by side, they looked more like sisters than mother and daughter. They had the same slight frame, slender waist, and sparkling blonde hair.

"Minnie is only a year younger than I am, but she's small. Sometimes she seems positively tiny, and I guess I've always envied her for that quality. Years ago I secretly nicknamed her Minnie Mouse, but I've never called her that to her face. I just sort of keep it in reserve.

"Most of the food preparation was done, so my mother

told me to go into the living room and call my father for dinner. He sort of indicated to me, that he'd be right there without ever taking his eyes off the television. He had recently developed a talent for talking to people without ever looking at them.

"We all took our places at the table. As usual Minnie sat next to my mom, and I placed myself at my father's side. But I don't want to give you the wrong impression; divisions in my family were never really hard and fast. As my mother placed the casserole of baked ziti on the table, she rested her hand on my shoulder and gently kissed the top of my head. I love my mother, and I've always wanted desperately to please her, but I've just never seemed to be everything she wanted me to be.

"Dinner proceeded pleasantly enough that evening. Mom chatted with dad. I helped myself to a generous portion of salad but went easy on the blue cheese dressing. I was determined to watch my weight now. If I cut out bread and dessert, I thought that maybe I could shed five pounds in a week or so.

"And then it happened. The words came softly enough from my mother's mouth, but they stung my ears like a thousand needles. My mother simply turned to my father and said, 'Marvin, guess what lovely girl is going to 'Cupid's Follies' this year with David Sockoloff? You remember the Sockoloffs, don't you? They own the Bella Fashion outlets in Westchester.'

"It was as if I couldn't hear my mother's voice any longer. Her words were just background sounds now. David Sockoloff was one of the handsomest, most popular boys at school. And my 'pretty skinny little Minnie sister' had asked him to 'Cupid's Follies.' And what was even more remarkable, he had accepted.

"I asked my sister how she did it, how she ever got enough courage to ask gorgeous David Sockoloff, whom practically everyone in the entire school wanted to go out with, to 'Cupid's Follies.' I couldn't believe it. David Sockoloff had accepted Minnie's invitation. I had heard he was going out with some college girl.

"Minnie's answer practically sent me through the floor. She flashed one of her beautiful sparkling smiles and said, 'I didn't ask him. Dave asked me.' I told her that was impossible, that everyone knew 'Cupid's Follies' was a girl-ask-boy dance. Minnie said she knew that, but added that Dave had said he had wanted to go out with her for such a long time that he was willing to defy custom. She told me he had said that he thought it would be cute for their first date to be on Valentine's Day.

"I didn't need or want to hear anymore. I just sat there hoping that Minnie wouldn't continue. I couldn't stop thinking about the way my own life was going. I didn't know why no one had asked me out in six months. And I didn't know why one of the most desirable boys at school was panting after my little sister Minnie Mouse. I only knew that my sister was petite, pretty, and wore a size four. Funny rhymes kept repeating through my mind— skinny Minnie, tiny, pretty. I couldn't seem to think straight, but I made myself try. I somehow had to get through dinner.

"That night dinner seemed to go on forever. It seemed like an endless ordeal. I felt so strange. Usually, when I'm upset, nothing seems to soothe me as much as potato chips, french fries, or a hot fudge sundae; actually anything palatable would fit the bill. But that night I was having a difficult time forcing my mother's marvelous baked ziti down my throat. I succeeded in finishing most of it, though, leaving a little bit to allow me to escape my mother's usual chiding for stuffing myself. I was always regarded as the size nine monster of the family.

"After about forty-five minutes, I was finally able to

escape to my room. I went to my bookcase and quickly pulled out all my old issues of *Seventeen* magazine. The exceedingly slender models were beautiful; they seemed to dance across the pages. To me, they seemed like an assortment of exquisite Minnie Mice.

"I'll never forget that night. More than ever, I wanted to be slender, very slender. That night I wanted 'Cupid's Follies' and David Sockoloff, and perhaps most of all I wanted to be my mother's favorite daughter. And I thought that if being thin would give me a chance to have it all, then I'd have to be thin. I became determined to stick to my diet this time, no matter what it cost.

"The next day was Saturday. I decided to go to the library to see what I could read about dieting and exercise. The public library didn't open until ten o'clock, but I stood outside the building at ten minutes of ten hoping to persuade the guard to let me in ahead of time. When that didn't work, I waited politely until the library formally opened and then sped directly to the section on weight reduction. It was marvelous. There were shelves and shelves of volumes on the subject. I thought there must be millions of other fat people just like me in Westchester, trying desperately to lose weight. I never dreamed there'd be so many books on shedding fat.

"I've always been a good student. If the teacher tells the class to read a chapter of the text, I don't feel secure reading the assignment just once; I usually read it three times over. Now I attacked the wealth of dieting information with the same vigor. It took me about three and a half hours to scan practically every text available. I remember how I hurriedly discarded books on good eating and forming a sound nutritional program. I selected only the books that promised to teach me how to take off pounds and inches instantaneously.

"I was carrying a load of books in each arm and was

walking toward the check-out desk when I saw Miss Waldorff coming out of her office. Miss Waldorff was now the library's director, but before she became the director, she worked at our library as the children's librarian. When I was very little, Miss Waldorff had always been my favorite person.

"I had always wanted to be just like her. I had even given some thought to becoming a librarian because of Sara Waldorff. Miss Waldorff is over six feet tall and has shiny red hair that hangs to her waist. She has a wonderful smile that always puts people at ease. The kids all love Miss Waldorff. She calls the children's section of the library the Magic Room and the kids who use it her little folk.

"When I was younger, Miss Waldorff planted a cardboard lollipop tree in the middle of the room, and after reading six books, you were permitted to pick a pop. She told stories to the three- and four-year-olds on a ruffled bedspread, which she called her magic carpet. I loved her because she always saved the best horse stories for me.

"That day when I saw Miss Waldorff, I ran up to her waving a book in each hand. I remember that she seemed surprised to see me with books on weight control. She said that I didn't need to lose any weight, that I had a beautiful figure already. She did mention that she was glad to see me reading, but added that I needed to read, not to diet.

"I left the library feeling elated. I wondered if Miss Waldorff had really meant what she said. Did somebody, especially somebody like Sara Waldorff, think I had a terrific figure? I wanted to believe that I was pretty, but I couldn't. And I wasn't willing to take any chances either. I remember that by the time I left the library it was past two-thirty and I hadn't eaten anything all day. I had walked to the library that morning in an effort to burn up calories, and I walked all the way home, hoping to use up even more energy.

"It took over a week before anyone noticed it, but at last I was able to savor the results of my diet. I stepped off the bathroom scale one morning wearing only a pair of panties and a smile. I hadn't eaten breakfast yet; in fact I hadn't even taken a sip of water. I always wanted to be at my thinnest when I weighed myself.

"The scale reading delighted me. I had gone from one hundred sixteen pounds to one hundred seven. But the most thrilling part of all was that the weight loss really showed. Now my size nine jeans swam on me. I could actually slide them off without unbuttoning them or even unzipping them. My long-cherished red silk dress looked like a tent on me. I had worn it the other day, and my friend's mother, who is a skilled seamstress, had offered to take it in for me.

"As the days passed, I seemed to spend more time than ever in front of my full-length mirror. My differing feelings about myself and the way I looked seemed to flitter through my mind endlessly. At times I imagined that I was pretty, even a bit glamorous. But in spite of my recent weight loss, most of the time I was still unhappy with my appearance. I just felt fat. Usually in the past I had found it very difficult to control my weight. But now somehow I firmly believed that if I could control my weight, then I would be able to control the rest of my life, and then things would finally go right for me.

"I began giving up my daily after-school candy bar. Then I stopped riding home on the school bus. I jogged for a short part of the three-mile trip, and then I walked briskly for most of the rest. It made for a very long and lonely trip home.

"These long walks home proved to be a very interesting

paradox. My energetic pace helped me to burn up calories, but it also made me feel famished. One night as I opened the front door I could smell my mother's homemade garlic bread baking in the oven. Dinner hour at my house had changed somewhat since my stringent diet went into effect. My mother, who in the past had warned me not to overeat, now seemed to respond to my diet program as if it were almost a personal challenge to her absolute authority.

"Every evening my mother now took pains to prepare my favorite foods. She made certain always to create an enticing dessert that would be difficult to refuse. Some evenings she'd even whip up some special taste treat just for me. One night she brought a plate of freshly made marshmallow fudge up to my room while I was studying. I thanked her, waited until after she left, and then fed the still warm chocolate morsels to my dog, Skipper. It seemed as if my mother and I had found a new battle ground. Each of us was proving to be a worthy opponent.

"One night my mother practically exploded at the dinner table. She saw me picking at my lasagna and garlic bread and threw down her napkin in disgust. My mother claimed that I was making her sick. She went on to complain that I didn't eat my food and that I was already starting to look like a scarecrow. She said that I didn't look good any more in even my nicest outfits.

"I pleaded with her to leave me alone, telling her that I simply couldn't eat any more. I looked up at my father for support but saw that none was forthcoming. Instead, my mother harshly continued, saying, 'Young lady, you will remain in your seat until you finish your meal. Don't open your mouth again unless it's to take another bite of food.'

"I knew better than to defy my mother once an argument had reached this point. I chewed slowly and swallowed my lasagna. I remember that it tasted like sawdust to me. It took four glasses of water to get it all down.

"When the meal was finally over, I excused myself and went to my room. I took off my clothes and put on my blue terry-cloth robe. I knew what I had to do now, and I headed straight for the bathroom.

"I turned on the water faucet full blast to muffle any sounds that might have carried from the room. I stripped off my robe, lifted the toilet seat, bent over the bowl, and stuck my finger down my throat as far as I could reach. I gagged and felt the nausea permeate my body as I vomited. My throat felt scratched, and my stomach muscles ached, but I repeated the process until I felt certain that I had thrown up all I had eaten.

"I flushed the toilet to rinse away what I had done. At last it was over, I thought as I sat down on the toilet bowl to relax. But was it? I couldn't be sure, but I thought my body might smell of vomit. I quickly jumped into the shower and scrubbed myself with lemon-scented soap until my skin began to flush pink.

"That night as I lay in bed trying to fall asleep, my mother came into my room. As she sat down on my bed, she asked if I was still awake. She told me that she was sorry she was cross with me at dinner and that she only wanted me to eat and be healthy. She said that I would always be her little girl.

"As my mother sat on my bed stroking my hair, the only thing I could think of was that I had just received another loving message from my mother who always seemed to be angry at me. At that moment I didn't know whether my mother really loved me or not, but I did know that I wanted my mother's love more than anything in the world.

"Still, I felt that I just couldn't give in to her then. I didn't want to eat. I desperately felt that I couldn't afford to be fat. But to please my mother I told her that every-thing was all right between us and that I knew she really cared about me. I reminded her that in the end I had been obedient and she had won. I had done as she asked and had finished everything on my plate.

"But after my mother left the room, I felt a strange sense of pride surge through me. I had been victorious; no one could force me to eat. I knew my dinner was now floating somewhere in a sewer."

TAKE IT AWAY

The anorectic is on an endless diet. A normal dieter will go through a period of self-denial and will then experience relief when at last he or she reaches the weight goal. But the anorectic persists, and the longer she continues her starvation regime, the more abnormal and deranged her thinking patterns may become.

Usually the anorectic remains inflexible in her stance. Her entire life is governed by the harsh application of a rigidly controlled set of rules regarding the intake and elimination of food from her body.

It is extremely difficult to diagnose anorexia nervosa at its onset. A slightly overweight person begins what appears to be a routine diet, but somehow in this process develops an unnatural fixation on food and body weight. A patient may have lost fifteen or twenty pounds and may just be starting to appear underweight when her physician begins to realize that she has no intention of giving up what has become an obsession with her. The change in body weight that makes the problem apparent can take place in only three or four months. If the condition is allowed to persist without treatment, anorectic behavior may become a way of life.

Rigid dieting is reinforced when the girl discovers others expressing concern for her. She may suddenly become the center of attention, and the experience can be quite flattering.

Perpetuating the anorectic state is not easy for the victim. The afflicted individual does not automatically adhere to the rigid standards she has devised for herself. Being an anorectic requires a good deal of effort on her part. She has put herself under a unique type of pressure, and the work is difficult. She has to starve herself continually, coping with constant hunger, while she must defend her choice to those around her almost daily.

The longer the anorectic remains untreated, the more firmly she may come to believe that she is a special person accomplishing an extraordinary goal. She lives in a private world in which she believes herself to be intrinsically superior. After a time, the anorectic may come to believe that she can no longer communicate with others who either can't or won't understand her purpose.

She may begin to withdraw and become increasingly isolated. In this way she further deprives herself of the normal experiences young people encounter in the everyday world. Eventually she may become completely absorbed in her pursuit of starvation. Thoughts of food and weight control will dominate almost her every thought. This type of separation can have a tragic effect on her long-range development. Unless psychotherapy or another method of treatment is introduced to help her view the world in a more realistic manner, she may remain anorectic for years.

Many anorectics develop strange misconceptions about their biological functioning. They will rigidly adhere to these notions despite any efforts on the part of others to make them see reality. Although one anorexia victim was a biology major at a well-known university in the West, she continuously insisted that she was afraid to put anything into her body for fear that it would never come out, but would just remain there extending her stomach and causing her to look fat.

Although she knew intellectually that this was impossible, she somehow could not shake her belief that this would happen to her. Like many anorectics, she claimed that she felt comfortable only when her stomach was completely flat.

An ironic behavioral symptom that the anorectic indulges in is binge eating. It may seem unusual that young girls who appear so frightened of taking in food at times feel uncontrollably compelled to ingest very large quantities of food. Yet in over 90 percent of the cases of anorexia nervosa, this symptom appears.

Once the anorectic has eaten the foods that she believes are forbidden to her, she may find herself in a state of extreme psychological discomfort. She may hate herself for being so weak as to have given in to a craving. The food that was so tempting to her less than ten minutes before becomes abhorrent now. She imagines that it will make her put on weight immediately, weight that will cause her to look fat, and she feels that there is almost no way in which she'll be able to take it off. She feels frightened, out of control, and terrified by the reality that she has actually eaten a good deal of fattening food. She has put herself under extreme stress, and she relieves herself of this burden by forcing herself to throw up.

The kinds of binges employed by anorectics vary greatly. Once this pattern of binge eating and regurgitation is established, however, it is extremely difficult to overcome.

Marci was an anorectic whose binges centered on sweets. It was not unusual for her to consume six or seven pounds of chocolate, one or two cakes—generally either cherry cheese or seven layer—and then perhaps a quart of ice cream. After such an extensive intake of food, Marci found that throwing up was both mentally and physically comforting.

Although this quantity of food may sound exceptionally large, it is not unusual for an anorectic to consume at least this amount and even much more. Another speciality of Marci's was eating peanut butter directly out of the jar with a spoon. It was not unusual for her to eat five or six jars in one sitting.

Linda, on the other hand, liked the idea of eating sumptuous meals without putting on any weight. She would go into a diner near her home and order a fruit cup as an appetizer, a deluxe burger platter, a coke, and a hot fudge sundae for dessert.

Too embarrassed to order additional food there, she would request the same menu at the four other diners in her town in one afternoon. She tried the same technique with more elaborate types of food, but found that her newly acquired habit was just too costly to keep up. When she had used up her allowance and spent what little savings she had in the diner, Linda was forced to prepare these large meals for herself at home. She always cooked when there was no one else in the house, and she always threw up immediately afterward.

Regurgitation on a continuous basis is not as simple as it sounds. Most of the girls soon find that in addition to ingesting large quantities of food, they also have to drink quarts of fluids in order to bring it all up easily. Since many of the anorectics have always gone to great lengths to appear to be perfect young ladies for whom this habit of throwing up might appear unsanitary and unhealthy, they often become quite ashamed of this behavior, which they are forced to pursue with utmost secrecy.

This habit can become chronic and more serious with the passage of time. The anorectic may come to feel the need to regurgitate even after eating only a small amount of food. She still may try to expel "every last bite of food."

If the anorectic cannot secure the privacy to complete her purging ritual, she may feel uneasy. In a busy household, for example, someone may constantly need to use the bathroom. Even if the anorectic cannot find the opportunity to regurgitate until hours after she has binged, when most of the food has left her stomach, she will do so. She firmly believes that this rutual is her only defense against becoming fat.

The typical anorectic usually becomes a chronic exercise addict as well as a dieter. She knows that an extreme exercise ritual followed consistently will burn up calories, and that is her goal. The anorectic also believes that a vigorous exercise program will help to firm her body, and indeed many of these girls do come to look like well-toned skeletons.

Jessica, a fourteen-year-old anorectic from Cleveland, got up every morning at five o'clock to run two miles around the park before eating her breakfast of one saltine cracker and three glasses of water.

Nina, a seventeen-year-old anorectic who had at one time shown some interest in studying dance, begged her parents to increase her dancing lessons from one to four weekly sessions. Hoping that giving in to their daughter's whim might encourage her to eat, Nina's parents agreed. She also convinced them to mirror the recreation room and install exercise bars.

Nina began to practice dance in earnest. She danced

every day after school for hours and then for a number of additional hours after dinner. She would stop only when her parents forced her to go to bed.

But Nina found that many nights she felt anxious and was unable to sleep. She was afraid that if she stopped exercising to sleep, she might put on weight. This fear grew so real for Nina that on many nights after her parents had gone to bed, she would go down to the recreation room and dance without music so as not to wake anyone. Sometimes she danced until two or three in the morning. She would then try to sleep for a few hours and rise at six to dress for school.

Nina continued her day and night dancing ritual for more than six months. She danced and starved herself from one hundred five pounds to sixty-four pounds. One day her sister found her lying unconscious on the floor of the recreation room. She had collapsed from malnutrition and exhaustion.

Elizabeth was a victim of anorexia nervosa who took advantage of every opportunity to exercise. Although she lived over four miles from her school, she gave up riding the school bus both ways and walked instead to burn up calories. Elizabeth became extremely active in school sports and also enrolled in a gymnastics club. She discovered that it was very difficult for her to sit still. She exercised while lying in bed at night, while taking a shower, and even found exercises she could perform undetected while sitting at her desk in class.

Debbie, a sixteen-year-old girl suffering from anorexia nervosa, worked out her own personal exercise regime, which she dubbed her training program. Debbie claimed that she was training to get in shape, but as she continued to lose weight, others felt that she was beginning to look emaciated and that her diligent exercise program was probably having a negative effect on her health.

Every morning when Debbie woke up she did two hundred sit-ups, jumped rope, showered, avoided eating any breakfast, and then jogged to school. Her afternoon and evening exercise schedules were comparably stringent. Debbie promised herself never to go to sleep until one o'clock in the morning, as she firmly believed that she needed at least this amount of time to burn up any extra calories she may have stored.

Most anorectics soon become exercise faddists. Their fear of sitting still or of simply resting often tends to increase as the illness progresses. Some claim that for even some relief of their feeling of tremendous anxiety they attempt to keep themselves in a state of perpetual motion. Even if an anorectic is only wiggling her toes, she will feel that at least she is doing more for herself than remaining at ease. Many anorectics admit their fear that when they are motionless, they may not be burning up calories and in fact may even be putting on weight.

The anorectic becomes obsessed with the notion of eliminating food from her body. She feels guilty over any morsel of food that she may have allowed to enter her body in a moment of weakness. After eating, she may be filled with self-hatred. The unwanted food has got to come out, one way or another. In addition to self-induced vomiting, the anorectic will overdo the use of laxatives.

Many anorexia nervosa victims will take almost a whole package of laxatives a day, turning their elimination to liquid. Whether or not they have eaten at all during that day, many will still continue to take the laxatives in huge doses. Even the suggestion that any food may still lurk in their digestive systems is abhorrent to them.

The abuse of laxatives, so common a symptom in the anorectic, poses a serious threat to a person's health. For one thing, once the body becomes used to the effects of laxatives, it will stop functioning as it previously did without them. Now the body will no longer perform the elimination process naturally on its own. So if an anorectic takes laxatives for six months and then one day stops, she may find that she is unable to have bowel movements. In some cases, uneliminated waste becomes impacted in the large intestine and has to be removed surgically.

Often anorectics abuse diuretics, drugs that increase the body's production of urine, as well. Many anorectics drink large quantities of water or diet soda. They do this to help alleviate the sensation of hunger without ingesting anything caloric. This fluid intake also makes them feel bloated and full, however. In their irrational fear that they will remain that way and that somehow the fluid will not pass through them, they take large quantities of diuretics to aid the process.

Another serious health hazard posed by the misuse of diuretics and laxatives is that such abuse results in disturbances in the body's electrolyte balance. Severe imbalances may prove to be fatal unless corrected through intravenous infusion.

Chapter 6

THE ULTIMATE INTERVENTION

Anorexia nervosa is a complex psychological disorder. Ideally it might be successfully treated through psychotherapy or family therapy. In some instances, however, its effect on the biological functioning of its victim can be so devastating that more drastic measures have been resorted to in numerous cases.

The problem of how to get food into a starving patient who has directed her entire energy into a rigid determination not to eat presents an extremely difficult task. Force feeding is perhaps the most obvious answer, but it is not always the best choice, since the patient is already suffering from severe psychological problems. It is important to be certain that one is not inflicting any further damage. Unfortunately, some treatment strategies have amounted to little more than a battle of wills between two equally determined sides.

The initial tendency may be to treat the starvation symptoms, but in reality it is important to look at the totality of the individual involved. The eating problem is really just the surface problem of a person who lacks a sense of personal competence and control over her life and destiny.

Some doctors have recommended that the anorectic patient be hospitalized once her weight level drops to a severely low point and there appears to be no possibility of improvement without some type of intervention. Hospitalization has been as devastating in some cases as it has been successful in others.

Often physicians believe it is beneficial to treat a patient away from home, as many of the difficulties these girls face arise from their home situations. At times this procedure may be successful in merely adding poundage to the patient's body, but often it turns out to be a short-lived cure. The underlying problems regarding how the patient feels about herself and how she and her family interact with each other—problems that caused her to become ill initially—remain untouched.

The girl returns to her home as unable to deal with her environment as she was before she was admitted to the hospital. The symptoms reappear, and she begins once again to lose weight. At times the results may be so devastating that the patient drops below the weight level for which she was initially hospitalized.

Some anorectics have a continuous revolving-door experience with hospitals. When their weight drops to the point that their health is seriously jeopardized, they are admitted to a hospital. The patient is then induced to gain weight there by one means or another, only to be sent home where she once again sheds her newly acquired pounds. Some anorectics are hospitalized as often as every three or four months. Some people believe that this is the only way to keep these young girls alive.

Not every hospital is capable of dealing effectively with an anorectic, however. In an environment in which hospital staff is continually under pressure to save people who are ill through no fault of their own, a young girl who is blessed with naturally good health but who appears simply to be obsessed with aggravating everyone by deliberately starving herself may evoke little sympathy from those assigned to her care.

A hospital environment in which food and medication are prescribed and appropriate behavior is dictated may be a small improvement over the oppressive dictatorial home life the girl came from originally. If staff members are not adequately trained in providing psychiatric care, they may feel helpless and frustrated in the face of their patient's stubborn refusal to eat.

Often hospital staff feel inadequate to cope with the tricky and sometimes deceitful measures the anorectic feels compelled to resort to. One young nurse described her feelings this way: "I had just gotten out of nursing school and was really eager to help people when little Anna was admitted to our unit at the hospital. The other nurses thought of her as a rich spoiled brat, but Anna and I just seemed to take to each other. I couldn't help feeling sorry for her. She looked so skinny and drawn that she reminded me of a little starving sparrow.

"I was determined to make friends with her. I thought that if she felt that she had someone who was really on her side, she'd probably feel better about herself. And I hoped that I could convince her to eat for her own good. I went to great pains to help her learn to help herself.

"For about two weeks, I spent my lunch hours and breaks with her. I tried to convince her that we should eat together. She told me that she felt too nervous to eat in front of anyone, but she promised that she would eat her food after I left. She told me that she would eat because I had been so nice to her that she now felt there was finally someone she could trust.

"I checked her food trays every day. There was never any leftover food on them. I bought her special little sweet treats out of my own money. Cupcakes, cookies, ice cream sandwiches, and all kinds of candy bars. Anna thanked me continuously and said that I was a terrific pal.

"But as the days and eventually the weeks passed, we all realized that Anna wasn't putting on any weight. In fact, after two weeks of hospitalization Anna had actually lost two pounds. Then the truth came out. I guess at that point there was no sense in her trying to keep up the pretense any longer.

"Anna was too ashamed to face me, but her roommate told me that she had flushed the hospital food as well as my snacks down the toilet. She poured the soda I had bought her into the plant containers.

"I felt so deceived. I couldn't imagine how Anna could have been so dishonest and unfair. I guess she thought our friendship was a joke. The other nurses told me not to blame myself or to take Anna's stunts so personally.

"I know that these skinny kids are trained to be people-pleasers. Their parents demand complete obedience and conformity, and if the girls want any independence they think that they have to lie to get it. But when you try so hard to get through to one of them and her health and future come to mean so much to you, you don't appreciate being tricked.

"The whole experience became extremely frustrating. I stopped spending my spare time and money on Anna. I decided instead to put my energy into a patient who was genuinely sick and would appreciate my effort and concern. The day Anna weighed in at two pounds under what she had weighed when she came to us was the last day I ever spoke to her."

In actuality, Anna was genuinely ill, but the nurse was too hurt by what she regarded as Anna's betrayal of her friendship to realize just how sick the child was. Although the nurse initially had the best of intentions, she had no understanding of the complexity of Anna's disorder. She also lacked the endurance and perseverance necessary to make any progress with an anorectic.

Unfortunately, anorectics often come up against this reaction. Untrained or inexperienced, though often well intentioned, individuals do their best to get through to one of these girls and then overreact with anger and frustration when they learn that the patient has not dealt honestly with them. Often they develop a punitive attitude toward the patient who now comes to feel even more cut off and alienated than before they attempted to help.

In addition to the problem of hospital staff who are untrained to deal with this often frustrating illness, the question of whether or not hospitalization will be successful also depends on a number of factors. Among them are the girl's age, her current relationship with her parents, and the duration of her illness.

If the patient is young and the illness has not continued for an extended period of time, there is a more promising chance for recovery. Cooperative parents, who are willing to make changes in their lives and in the way they relate to other family members, are also an extremely important factor.

Hospitalization of an anorectic can be a tricky experience. Even if the patient develops a good relationship with her day nurse and dietitian, and even if she appears to be making some progress, a nurse on another shift who becomes frustrated with the patient's refusal to eat and subsequently becomes threatening and severe with the girl may seriously impede the headway made by other staff members.

If the patient is to benefit from a restful, noncoercive hospital experience, each member of the staff who interacts with her must demonstrate a consistently sympathetic approach.

A genuine recognition of the patient's tumultuous feelings and what she is actually going through is necessary as well. Under these circumstances, hospitalization may prove helpful in allowing the patient to begin to restore her health. It may also offer her a brief respite from a tense family situation.

In life or death situations, hospitalization of the anorectic patient may be the only choice. In some cases, severe and persistent starvation as well as disturbances in the girl's electrolyte balance brought about by the abuse of laxatives and diuretics may literally jeopardize the girl's survival. Such instances require that the patient be admitted to a hospital, and unfortunately, once she is hospitalized, drastic and often unpleasant measures may have to be initiated immediately.

Carol, an anorectic whose weight had fallen from one hundred twenty-six to seventy-six pounds, was taken to a hospital by ambulance after she collapsed during her gym class. Frantic about the possibility of putting on weight, Carol had been ingesting whole packages of diuretics and laxatives at a time. This dosage resulted in a severe loss of essential chemicals from her system and caused her to be dehydrated to a nearly fatal point. After she was hospitalized, the disturbance in her electrolyte balance was restored by intravenous infusion of solutions of minerals and glucose. Later she was given hospital food and advised to remain in the hospital. The dramatic intervention saved Carol's life, but she could hardly be thought to be cured.

Once hospitalized, anorectics often develop a heightened sense of fear over the prospect of ingesting any form of solid food. Some people believe that this fear may arise because the anorectic feels less in control in a hospital setting where there may be less opportunity for her to engage in strenuous exercise or excessive vomiting.

To ease the anorectic's anxiety, the hospital dietitian may order a rich nutritional fluid that is both flavorful and high in calories. Some anorectics have claimed that it is easier for them to drink than to chew. In addition, the dietitian may try to offer the anorectic patient some type of solid food as part of a gentle reintroduction to normal eating practices.

In the past, when a hospitalized anorectic refused to take any type of food voluntarily, the hospital staff may have resorted to forced tube feeding in order to save the patient's life. This method, however, can be extremely distressing to the patient psychologically. Often the patient experiences great humiliation at such blatant control of her body by others. At times these girls may leave the hospital feeling extremely depressed. At least two young women are known to have committed suicide after being tube fed by force.

Today if a hospitalized anorectic is near death and is still unable to eat, she probably will be nourished intravenously. In this way, the physician can be assured that the patient is not throwing away or throwing up food. This method is not foolproof, however. A resourceful anorectic will manage to jam up the machinery or even pull the tube out of her arm altogether. If she can manage to accomplish this surreptitiously, an anorectic patient may succeed in rejecting nourishment for a few hours until the nurse discovers the act and remedies the situation.

Hospitalization can never be anything more than a life-saving measure that will make possible long-term treatment commitments on the part of the patient and her family. Unfortunately, it sometimes takes hospitalization to force evasive families to deal with the fact that they are faced with a serious problem that is not going to disappear. The possible consequence is too severe not to be dealt with: their child could lose her life.

Once the patient's life is out of danger, some hospitals advocate a technique known as behavior modification in treating the anorectic patient. Doctors who use behavior modification see the anorectic's refusal of food as what they call an incorrect learned response. In helping their patients, they attempt to create an environment in which some positive relearning or reconditioning can take place. A system of rewards and punishments is set up between the patient and the hospital staff.

If the anorectic succeeds in gaining weight, she is rewarded. Something pleasant, agreed to by the patient and the therapist beforehand, will be given to the patient. The girl may be allowed to purchase some cosmetics from the hospital's gift shop, or she may be allowed to place an expensive long-distance call to a special friend or relative.

Following a behavior modification system, however, if the patient doesn't gain weight or if she should continue to lose weight, she can be assured of punishment. For example, the telephone or television may be taken out of her room, or she may be denied access to her favorite books. If the punishments are sufficiently unpleasant, the patient may force herself to eat if only so that she will be discharged from the hospital. Behavior modification as a form of therapy is most often successful if the patient comes to understand that she needs help and volunteers to cooperate with the therapist.

If the patient's health and nutritional level can be somewhat improved by any means through hospitalization, the patient will be in a better state to benefit from psychotherapy. No amount of nutritional advice will be genuinely helpful to an anorectic, however, unless the mental causes underlying the disorder are dealt with.

BULIMIA—THE SISTER SICKNESS

Bulimia is another eating disorder, which in many ways is quite similar to anorexia nervosa. Like anorexia, bulimia is rooted in psychological causes but can often result in serious medical complications as well.

Bulimia, which means an abnormal hunger, is sometimes referred to as the binge-purge syndrome. It is generally characterized by a significant eating binge that the victim deals with by means of self-induced purge. These binges occur because of food cravings that are rooted in psychological causes; they are not responses to genuine hunger.

A binge may take many varied forms. There are no standard foods that bulimics tend to use. The binges are as varied as are the young women who engage in this type of behavior. A bulimic may binge on favorite foods that she remembers fondly as having brought comfort to her during childhood. One woman cited hot cereal with real cream and lots of sugar as her favorite food to binge on. She claimed it reminded her of how her mother had stayed home from work to care for her whenever she became ill as a child. On these rare occasions, she was the fortunate recipient of her mother's undivided attention, and on such days her mother always prepared hot cereal for her in this manner.

Usually the foods used in an eating binge are not as clearly related to the individual's past, however. They are frequently the bulimic's favorite foods. These are often "forbidden" items, high in caloric content, which the person would try to deny herself if she were not on a binge. Ice cream, candy, popcorn, cake, and pizza are common favorites.

Some women binge by eating one meal on top of another. They routinely repeat the various courses: appetizer, entrée, and dessert. Others have specialty binges that they have devised to meet their own personal needs. One woman especially liked to eat a quart of rum raisin ice cream and then a jar of grape jelly, which she would eat with a spoon straight out of the jar. Next she'd devour a pint of vanilla fudge ice cream and a jar of apricot jelly. She liked to finish off the splurge with a bag of chocolate chip cookies.

Andrea, a twenty-four-year-old, claimed that she never intentionally planned what she binged on. She stated that she just fell prey to every inticing food place she passed on the way home from work. She'd first stop at the bakery where she'd buy a dozen jelly doughnuts and a chocolate cake. She'd eat the doughnuts on the way home and try to save the cake for later. Andrea's next stop was the candy store. Candy was sold by the pound there, and Andrea almost always purchased one or two pounds of chocolate-covered jellies. Some days she'd choose the orange jellies while at other times the raspberry jellies were her first choice.

Having satisfied her sweet tooth momentarily, Andrea

would stop at the local delicatessen. She'd usually buy a pound of ham and another pound of either roast beef or bologna. Delicious hot dogs were sold there, and Andrea always bought one or two, which she ate heartily topped with mustard, relish, and sauerkraut.

Her next stop was the local ice cream parlor where she'd have a double-scoop sprinkled sugar cone of the home-made flavor of the day. From there she would usual-ly head straight home, where she'd finish the chocolate cake she had bought on her first stop at the bakery. She generally washed the cake down with a quart or two of ginger ale.

Andrea had tried to convince herself and everyone else that there was no planned method to her eating binges. Yet she always stopped at the same stores where she bought and ate basically the same foods each working day. Even though she claimed that all of these stores were located along her route home, she actually had to go sev-eral blocks out of her way to visit them all each day. With-out realizing it, Andrea had worked these foods into her life. She had come to need and expect the comfort they afforded her, and she became extremely anxious at the thought of missing any of her favorite foods.

The amount of time spent binging as well as the extent of the binge varies among bulimic individuals. Some women are very careful about what they consume during the day. Because their work or school situation might not afford them an opportunity for purging, they might feel extremely uncomfortable eating even small amounts of food during the daytime. Instead, these individuals may prefer to delay eating any significant amount of food until evening when they are alone and can gorge and purge themselves in privacy.

A bulimic does not necessarily binge every day. Some do it only on weekends when they have adequate privacy to engage in their unusual ritual. Others may binge and purge only on extremely stressful occasions. Bulimics tend to follow patterns, but these patterns are subject to change. If the individual's life is altered in a meaningful way and she is experiencing difficulty coping with the change, an already established bulimic is likely to intensify her binge-purge behavior.

Karen, a twenty-five-year-old housewife who had recently returned to college to complete her education, began to engage in binge-purge behavior as a method of dealing with the stress she experienced when her husband clearly expressed his resentment of her going to school. Karen's husband believed that the time his wife spent attending classes and completing assignments could be put to better use caring for her home and children.

Karen felt genuinely torn. She wanted to be a good wife and mother, but she also wanted an education that would guarantee her an interesting career when her children grew older. Every time she enjoyed a lecture or felt satisfaction over completing an assignment successfully the feeling was always accompanied by an acute sense of guilt. Karen wanted to please her husband, her professors, her children, and herself simultaneously. She realized she had set a difficult goal for herself, and as a result she felt continually under extreme stress.

Karen had a life-long history of watching her weight. Even after having two children, she had managed to maintain a trim, attractive figure. She had a tendency to put on weight easily, however, and she felt that she almost always had to be on some sort of diet. She claimed that she loved to eat, but for most of her life she had gone to great pains not to give in to this pleasure.

Now under the pressure of a very personal internal struggle between her academic goals and her family obligations, Karen turned to food for comfort. She would take her lunch with her to school, eat it between classes, and then enjoy a second lunch with her classmates after the morning session. Karen also said that she had recently begun to experience an intense craving for sweets.

Every time she ate lunch, which was soon two to four times a day, she allowed herself to eat one or two packages of cupcakes or cookies for dessert. She also began to carry extra packages of cupcakes with her during the day.

At this point in her life, Karen felt as if she simply had to have the pastry. Eating afforded her pleasure in the midst of stress. Karen ate the cakes as she walked to her classes and as she rode the bus to and from school. Although eating was not permitted in the classroom, Karen sat in the back of the room and secretly slipped small pieces of cake from her handbag to her mouth as the professor lectured.

Within a short period of time, Karen found herself consuming a tremendous quantity of food daily. It had become common for Karen to eat over thirty cupcakes a day in addition to several large meals.

The whole experience proved to be devastating to the young woman. She had always cared about her appearance, but now she felt as if she had lost the willpower that had enabled her to resist overeating in the past. She felt out of control. Every day she woke up telling herself that today was going to be different: today she was not going to binge. Yet somehow her resolve did not hold out. She might be able to go for an hour or two without overeating, but the moment she began to feel anxious, she headed straight for the cookie jar.

As one would expect within a relatively short time Karen put on a significant amount of weight. She had difficulty fitting into her clothes, and she felt repulsed by her own image every time she looked into the mirror.

Karen began to hate herself for not having the control to stop binging, and she hated the way her enormous intake of food was beginning to make her look.

At about that time Karen's bulimia surfaced. She couldn't cope with her recent weight gain. Each time she overate, Karen was filled with disgust and self-recrimination. She was no longer able to deny her craving for food, but she was unable to deal with being overweight, so she began to force herself to regurgitate after binging.

At first, throwing up brought Karen a great sense of relief. She was able now to eat what she desired without facing consequences. Initially, Karen vomited only twice a day, once in a rest room at her college and again when she returned home. She soon found that the twice daily regurgitations were not sufficient, however. She was still consuming more calories than she burned up, and those extra calories were turning to fat.

Karen began to panic. She forced herself to vomit more frequently. If she couldn't find the privacy in which to complete this ritual, she faced severe bouts of anxiety. Karen found herself throwing up in the rest rooms of bus stations, school buildings, and restaurants. If someone heard her vomiting and asked if she was all right, Karen would say it was a virus or something she had eaten that didn't agree with her.

It wasn't long before Karen became ashamed of herself and of the purging rituals she felt compelled to perform. She knew that she was no longer behaving normally, but she felt too ashamed of what she was doing to explain her compulsion to anyone in order to get help.

Karen's behavior soon followed an easily discernible pattern: she had to eat enormous quantities of food in order to get through the day and she then had to purge the food from her body by regurgitating almost as soon as she had swallowed the last mouthful.

Karen's bulimia brought with it a whole new set of problems that she had to deal with on a daily basis. Karen now had a sore throat constantly from vomiting up to twenty times a day. The recurring regurgitation also caused her salivary glands to become infected and swollen, giving her face a round, puffy, bloated look.

When Karen wasn't near her home, she often felt compelled to throw up and had to use a public toilet. As a result, her clothes were sometimes stained by vomit. Often it stuck to her legs and shoes. Unfortunately, Karen usually came to smell like someone who had just vomited. Being away from home so many hours a day, she wasn't able to shower and change her clothing as often as would be appropriate under the circumstances.

In no way can a bulimic lead an anxiety-free life. She is not comfortable with binging and throwing up, yet she continuously feels that she must engage in such behavior. The psychological profile of a bulimic usually reveals low self-esteem. The victim lacks a deep sense of confidence and worth, and although she may exhibit a facade of cheerfulness, she actually harbors serious doubts about her capabilities and effectiveness as a human being.

A typical bulimic feels inadequate to cope with many situations, although she might not be fully conscious of these feelings at all times. When a problematic or hurtful situation arises in her life, she feels that she has to binge on high-calorie foods. She is unable to control this urge, and so she overeats. Almost immediately following the binge, she becomes disgusted with herself for giving in to her craving and believes that now she'll certainly put on weight. She forces herself to regurgitate, and only then is her immediate anxiety relieved.

The bulimic may never fully realize what she is actually putting herself through. She just feels the urge to binge; often she may not be aware that the urge appeared in response to some form of stress or anxiety that she may have just experienced. Even if she is conscious of the feeling or incident that provoked her irrational panic, she may believe that she lacks the resources to cope with the problem in a healthy and realistic manner. The binge-purge syndrome becomes a substitute mechanism for dealing with stress that she is unable to face directly.

Ironically, the binge-purge syndrome aids the anxiety-torn individual in still another way. She spends so much time and effort throughout the day eating to wash away her fears and then in purging that to some extent the bulimic isolates herself from the psychological process that triggered the binge originally. She becomes too absorbed in binging and purging to think about her other problems. As one bulimic explained, "It's hard to worry about not getting the promotion you want or being dumped by your boy friend once the whole cycle begins. If you're stuffing a sundae down your throat, you'll feel good, if only for a little while. Then the panic about getting it out of your stomach begins immediately. You don't have a chance to worry about anything but that now. You feel a short period of relief after you've thrown up. It's almost as though you've been saved once again from the worst consequence—getting fat.

"After that I usually clean the toilet bowl and start looking for something good to eat. In almost a matter of moments the whole process begins to repeat itself. You are really kept quite busy by this new dimension of your life. You don't have much time to give any real thought to other aspects of your life that may not be going as well as they could be."

Once a bulimic binge-purge syndrome has been established, it is extremely difficult to break without professional intervention. Some bulimics wake up each morning vowing that today they will not binge or purge. Unfortunately, however, such promises are often extremely short-lived.

If a bulimic experiences a relaxing, uneventful day, she may be able to control her urge to binge. To help herself through any stressful period, she might even consider allowing herself only one binge-purge episode in the evening.

The problem usually arises if there is some deviation in the day's schedule. Even a seemingly innocuous change can set the urge to binge and purge in motion.

A bulimic needs to feel that her existence is well under control. She tries to structure her life in order not to allow herself time to deal with the tremendous anxiety that she might become more conscious of if she faces a period of free time that has not been allotted to a particular activity or purpose. An unpleasant or unplanned incident or an unexpected period of time with nothing to do is sufficient to set off a binge that must eventually be purged. One binge may then lead to another and then still another. The anxiety that spurs the bulimic on may be so intense that she pushes all other activities aside until she has satisfied her urge to complete this ritual. She has long forgotten the promise she may have made to herself that morning not to get caught up in the cycle.

An unending cycle is initiated. The binge-purge syndrome becomes a way of relieving tension. The fears that grow out of the ritual itself—not having sufficient food to binge on or the privacy in which to vomit—only serve to add to the intensity of the problem.

Linda, a nineteen-year-old bulimic, described her feelings this way: "After about six months of being bulimic, the sickness just seemed to take over my life. I tried so hard to control the binges; eating so much frightened me. No matter how much I tried to throw up or how often, I was always afraid that I'd be unable to get all of the food out of me. I knew that if I became fat, I'd feel desperate. I don't believe I'd want to go on living.

"Time spent by myself has become about the most

frightening aspect of my life. I usually ride the express bus home from the college campus to my house every day. The bus leaves the college every twenty minutes. One day I stayed a few minutes after class to talk to a friend, and I missed the bus I usually catch. When I realized what had happened, I simply felt terrified.

"I panicked. No one could tell from the outside, but inside I felt terrible. It was as if I had become over-whelmed with anxiety, and there seemed to be no relief in sight. When I looked at the situation intellectually, it's difficult for me to comprehend why I felt as I did.

"After all, I knew that another bus would arrive in twenty minutes. There was a bench at the bus stop, and I could have sat there and waited for the vehicle to arrive. I certainly had enough homework to do to keep myself busy for more than twenty mintues, and I had all my books and notes with me.

"But it didn't happen that way. All of a sudden I felt ravenously hungry. I knew it wasn't really hunger: it felt more like a very strong craving for sweets. I recognized that I was about to binge, and I tried to control the impulse, but it was no use. I had to give in. I thought that if I ran to the campus candy store and was waited on quickly, I could be back in time to catch the next bus.

"When I reached the store, I felt even more out of control. I didn't know what to buy. I wanted to eat everything in sight. I chose seven candy bars, two packages of potato chips, and several cans of Coke. The store also sold ice cream, so I bought a double scoop of strawberry to eat on the way to the bus stop and had a quart packed for the bus ride home.

"I returned to the bus stop with about five minutes to spare, when I realized that the candy store clerk had not included a plastic spoon with which to eat the ice cream on the bus. What I felt was a combination of anger and terror. Even though I knew that most people did not devour quarts of ice cream right out of the container with a spoon, I felt that the clerk had been careless in not providing one.

"I tried to think how I could eat the ice cream without a spoon. I felt that it was too soft and sticky to eat with my fingers, yet not fluid enough to drink directly out of the container. And besides, I felt it might be too embarrassing to drink a quart of strawberry ice cream out of its container by myself on the bus. Not that I hadn't done it before, but it usually drew a few unflattering comments from the other bus passengers.

"I still had a few minutes before the bus was scheduled to arrive. I thought that if I ran all the way to the store and back, I might be able to pick up the spoon and still catch the next bus. I knew I didn't have very much time, but I decided to give it a try.

"As you might imagine, I missed that bus. By the time I returned to the bus stop from the store, the bus had already departed. I felt depressed and anxious at the same time. I decided to try to wait for the next bus. That meant I had another twenty minutes to deal with. I sat down on the bus stop bench and began to devour the candy bars, potato chips, ice cream, and soda I had bought.

"I polished off my enormous snack in under ten minutes. I felt very full, and my stomach was distended, but at the same time I wanted more food. It would take another ten minutes for the next bus to arrive, and I felt anxious about having nothing to do and nothing to eat while I waited.

"I decided to solve the problem in a manner that had become typical of the way I had recently become accustomed to handling tense situations. I decided to catch a still later bus home. Meanwhile I walked a few blocks to my favorite Chinese restaurant for a full-course dinner. I used to feel uncomfortable eating whole meals in restaurants by myself, but I soon overcame my inhibition, and I was now able to sit down at a table alone and order just about anything I wanted.

"The meal was delicious. Even though I already felt uncomfortably full as I sat down to eat it, I thoroughly enjoyed every morsel. At one point between the appetizer and the main course, I thought about going to the ladies' room to throw up so that I'd be able to eat still more. I soon discovered, however, that the ladies' room was out of order and closed.

"At first I felt a bit anxious. I always like to know that there's a place where I can vomit within minutes, but I promised myself that I'd throw up the minute I reached my apartment—which of course is exactly what I did.

"I know that what I'm saying must sound ridiculous to you. Some people to whom I've confided the truth have even laughed out loud. But it really isn't funny to me. After all, it's my life; yet I feel as if I am being controlled by some outside force that makes me a victim of this binge-purge thing.

"Almost every day I tell myself that once and for all this behavior has got to end. As things stand now I feel like a freak. I tell myself that I have to learn to eat and act normally. Then something happens to me and I give in to the urge. It's as though I'm the victim of a horrible habit that I just can't break. There doesn't seem to be an easy answer. I keep wondering how long this is going to go on."

Madelyn, a twenty-one-year-old bulimic from Boston, had similar feelings about unstructured time. To quote her, "Nothing frustrates me more than empty spaces. I need an activity to complete or someone to be with for almost every minute of my life. Of course, having someone around all the time has its negative side as well. If you feel that you have to binge, it's embarrassing to eat all that food in front of the person, and often it's even more difficult to extricate yourself from that individual when you need some time and privacy in which to vomit.

"Every day I make up a list of what I plan to do during that day. I try to structure everything, because I just can't deal with surprises. Even positive surprises always seem to trigger a binge. Although I'm not always aware of all my feelings, each day is sort of frightening to me. My main goal is just to get through each day. I don't want to sound as if I'm terribly unhappy and am just waiting around for old age and subsequent death. It's not that way at all. I don't usually feel miserable, just very frightened and anxious.

"It has become almost impossible for me to remain at home alone with nothing to do. I need an all-encompassing activity. If I don't have something I can really sink myself into, then all at once I feel nervous. Reading a book or watching television is not enough. I have to be constantly stimulated or there's always the danger of my running down to the corner grocery store and practically buying them out.

"It's as if I simply have to block out any potentially disturbing thoughts. There are times when I'm at home alone and I just feel a sort of free-floating anxiety. I can't say exactly what's bothering me; I just feel uneasy. I try talking to a friend on the phone. After that I'll usually try to immerse myself in an activity like cleaning out my closet or polishing my silver. Often it helps to play the radio and television simultaneously. The noise helps to block out my thoughts. It might work—the scary feelings may be pushed away—but more often I just have to binge."

"Purging" is the term used to describe the method the bulimic turns to in order to rid herself of the excessive food she has consumed on an eating binge. So far the method cited has been self-induced regurgitation, but most bulimics avail themselves of other means as well.

Like anorectics, bulimics constantly make excessive use of diuretics and laxatives. These women associate comfort with a sense of emptiness after binging. One bulimic claimed that she took between thirty and forty laxative tablets a day because she wasn't certain that throwing up alone would get it all out of her body. Another characteristic that bulimics share with anorectics is the tendency to exercise excessively. The same anxiety that compels these women to gorge also compels them to attempt to shed the calories they've consumed in any manner possible.

One very attractive nineteen-year-old bulimic had signed up for a different exercise class on each of five consecutive nights of the week. She claimed that in addition to helping her burn off calories, the classes also helped her to occupy her time and took her mind off the things that troubled her.

Unfortunately, the classes ended at eight-thirty in the evening, which provided sufficient time for several binges before the woman went to bed. To guard against this possibility, she began to invite several of her girl friends over after class to continue to exercise to music with her in her den.

This did not work as well as she had hoped, however. For one thing, most of her friends did not continue to join her after a few days, claiming that they had better things to do than execute fifty sit-ups every night. Two other friends, who did not share her bulimic compulsion, simply claimed that the regime was too strenuous.

To make matters still worse, the young woman was a chemistry major at an extremely demanding college. Her grades began to drop sharply as she continued to spend more time doing jumping jacks than she did on lab experiments. She realized what was happening to her, but claimed that she was unable to stop. She felt overcome by a need to keep moving.

Bulimics also often manage to starve themselves for brief periods of time. If they are able to ward off effectively the binge-purge behavior for a day or two, they may be able to fast or to eat next to nothing during that period. These short respites from eating actually turn into a different type of purge.

Bulimia is related to anorexia nervosa in still another way. Some women coming out of anorexia through professional treatment or by their own means unfortunately fall into the binge-purge syndrome. Instead of continuous starvation, they turn to binging and purging as a new means of controlling their weight. The term *bulimarexia* is used to describe this condition. It's a combination of the terms *bulimia (bulim)* and *anorexia (exia)*.

Although girls who have moved from anorexia to bulimarexia may look normal because they no longer have the skeletonlike appearance and generally seem to be closer to a normal weight, they have actually not taken a step toward sound mental health. They are still emotionally troubled victims of a binge-purge syndrome that is largely out of their control.

Many bulimics, however, never experience a prolonged period of self-induced starvation. These girls have always remained at approximately normal weight for their height and build. The longest they are able to go without food is one or two days. They control their weight through compulsive binging and purging. For this reason, anorexia and bulimia are viewed as psychological disorders that have a good deal in common, but are still separate and distinct conditions.

Although some men develop bulimia, the illness occurs much more frequently in women, most commonly during the late teen or early adulthood years. It is not uncommon, however, to find women in their thirties, forties, and even fifties who have recently turned bulimic.

One common trait that almost all bulimics share is a preoccupation at some former stage in their lives with their weight as it affected their physical appearance. Most bulimics have tried every type of fad diet, read all the latest diet books, and at one time or another taken diet pills.

Monica, an eighteen-year-old anorectic from Washington, D.C., described her history this way: "I'm just one of those people who has just sort of been on a diet all my life. I was kind of chubby as a child, but as soon as I turned twelve and realized that boys weren't interested in fat girls, I began what turned out to be practically a lifelong diet. That summer I went away to camp. The counselors never really watched what we ate. I guess they really didn't care. The camp had its own apple orchard, and the campers were allowed to pick whatever we wanted. There were plenty of apples in the camp meals as well. They were always serving apple pie, apple cobbler, or fruit salad.

"That summer I decided to skip the camp food and begin my own self-styled diet. I limited my daily food intake to five apples, which I picked myself. I tried to space the apples throughout the day, so I'd have one whenever I became hungry. By the end of the summer, I had lost eighteen pounds.

"I felt slim and beautiful. The only problem was that my hair had begun to thin and fall out. To this day I don't know whether or not that happened because of poor nutrition, but I suspect that might have had something to do with it, as my hair began to replenish itself when I returned home and resumed a normal diet.

"For the remainder of my teen years I was a victim of what is frequently referred to as the yo-yo syndrome. That means that my weight kept fluctuating up and down like a yo-yo.

"Each year I'd try to lose ten pounds right before summer so that I would look all right in a bathing suit. I was usually able to do that, but by the time Thanksgiving came around, I had always regained the weight. It was discouraging, but I sort of came to accept the ups and downs on my bathroom scale as an inescapable fact of life.

"Keeping my weight under control was not something I accomplished gracefully and with ease. I always had to be on guard to watch what I ate. My fear was that one day I would lose control totally and blow up like a balloon. I had never had a surplus of boy friends, and I felt that would finish me off altogether. I used to play a special little game with myself in order to keep my weight down. I'd set a weight goal for myself, and then I'd weigh myself every day to make certain I was on target. As soon as the scale registered three pounds above my goal, I'd initiate a starvation diet.

"I was rarely able to maintain my diet for any considerable length of time, but I usually managed to eat little enough to return to my weight goal. At that point I'd usually abandon any thought of restricting my food intake, and the whole process would begin again. As a result, I spent most of my life either overeating or trying to starve myself. I don't think I ever ate normally.

"I think that I must have read every diet book ever written and tried each diet advocated by the various authors. Our house is also extremely well stocked with diet foods. We've found a sugarless substitute for almost any item you can think of. My greatest wish is somehow to magically turn into a naturally slender person, to be able to eat whatever I desire without having to worry about it showing up on my thighs and hips a few days later.

"I always wished that I could be casual about food. I'd

like to be able to skip a meal without imagining that it's the end of the world. It would be wonderful to possess a well-toned, trim body with ease. But that just hasn't been my fate. I've always had a problem restricting my food intake, and I suspect that I always will.''

Bulimics characteristically remain at their normal weight. There is generally not a good deal of deviation within that range; some bulimics are only about five pounds over or under their ideal weight. In contrast, however, many women who suffer from bulimarexia are substantially thinner.

Recent studies have shown that bulimia is on the rise. Statistics gleaned from colleges across the country indicate that bulimia may be reaching near-epidemic proportions, with well over 35 percent of the young women on campus demonstrating some bulimic symptoms.

While anorexia is often thought of as the disorder of middle- and upper-class young women, the incidence of bulimia appears to be spreading across both income and class lines. There is nothing genetic about this disorder. Given the necessary attitude and circumstances, anyone could become bulimic. Yet not everyone does.

Like anorectics, bulimics definitely share some common traits. The Associates for Bulimia and Related Disorders in New York City describes the typical bulimia victim as follows:

"Bulimics are usually well-groomed, attractive, outgoing young ladies who do not appear to have a significant weight problem. Thousands of American women between adolescence and mid-adulthood have this disorder. Most bulimics are overly concerned with a perfect presentation of themselves.

"They suffer from low self-esteem and disproportionate need for validation from important others. This perfect facade masks underlying needs and emotional discomfort. They are sensitive to rejection and are often bewildered when their perfect presentation does not result in the acceptance they are looking for. They turn to food as a means of nurturing themselves, perhaps turning from the outer world in anger or disappointment.

"The binging is initially a pleasurable release from the unusual control and constant self-monitoring. However, the overeating is immediately followed by guilt, shame, and remorse; thus the purging. The purge begins a renewed drive for perfection and initiates yet another false attempt at controlling one's world.

"Bulimics are not only unassertive victims in their relationships with others (whom they continually try to please) but are also victims of the binge-purge cycle, which for many totally controls their lives."

Bulimics are usually obsessed with perfection—physical perfection as well as perfection in everything they attempt to accomplish. They tend to set unrealistically high standards for themselves, and when they fail to attain these lofty goals, they are often the first to condemn themselves loudly. No matter how hard these young women try, they never believe that they are quite good enough.

Lynn is a twenty-four-year-old bulimic who always appeared to succeed at everything with a minimum of effort. She had recently left the publishing house where she had been employed for five years to accept a highly paid, prestigious position with a New York public relations firm. When she left her publishing job, she was offered a contract to write a nonfiction book for her former boss. He had stated that Lynn was simply "too talented to lose altogether."

Last year Lynn also had the good fortune to marry a very attractive widower with an adorable young daughter. Everyone thought Lynn must be thrilled to have done so well in both her professional life and her personal life.

Lynn, however, was not at all delighted with her accomplishments. She confided to her mother that her new position was too stressful and that if her old company had had the sense to offer her the book contract last year, she would not have felt forced to leave her former position in search of something that offered more potential for the future. Lynn loved her new husband very much, but she secretly felt that her stepdaughter was a selfish, sloppy, arrogant child, who resented Lynn's presence in her father's home.

Everyone who knew her felt that Lynn had the world in the palm of her hand, but Lynn believed that she should have done much more with her life. She was extremely disappointed in herself, and as a result, she spent most of her evenings overeating and then throwing up.

Most bulimics are obsessed with receiving acceptance and approval from other people. They'll often go to inordinate means to please their teachers, supervisors, and friends. A bulimic is extremely careful always to do the right thing. She will suppress her own feelings in order to make the correct impression, and in many instances she may not even be conscious of what she actually wants for herself. The bulimic is so concerned with being a paragon of excellence in the opinion of others that she loses touch with her own feelings and goals.

This overwhelming need to be a people-pleaser places the bulimic in an extremely difficult position. She forces herself to look to others daily for confirmation that she is a worthwhile human being.

By virtually placing her own self-evaluation in the hands of others, the bulimic positions herself at the whim of other people. If her supervisor has a bad day and unjustly criticizes her, the bulimic may very well spend an hour in the ladies' room crying over the incident. Even if circumstances clearly indicate that she is not in the wrong, the bulimic will probably still blame herself. She takes every criticism to heart; she doesn't really trust herself, and she believes she has no standard against which to evaluate herself, except the opinion of others.

Carol, a twenty-one-year-old bulimic from Houston, Texas, began her first job as a high school English teacher the September after she graduated from college. Carol was determined to be a success at her job and to be well liked by everyone at school, but she soon found that this was a more difficult task than she had imagined.

Carol wanted to please her principal and at the same time follow the directions of her department head, but the two men were rarely able to see eye to eye on any issue, and Carol often found herself trapped in the middle. If she sided with one, she might incur the wrath of the other, and Carol was determined to avoid that at all costs. As a result she found herself in a constant state of anxiety. Carol began binging and purging whenever she found adequate privacy.

Carol found it difficult to relate to her students as well. She wanted to stimulate and challenge them, and she hoped they would see her as a friend as well as a teacher. Within weeks, however, Carol realized that her students were not interested in having her as their friend. They also seemed to have little interest in learning anything. They had each other's company and viewed Carol as not very much more than another authority figure who required them to complete and turn in homework assignments.

Carol felt frustrated by the situation. She had studied for four years to become a teacher, and now she felt as if she had failed at her lifelong goal. Her anxiety accelerated. The symptoms of her bulimia consequently intensified. She found that she now needed to binge and purge almost continuously.

At first she began to take days off from school, claiming

that she was sick, in order to give herself ample opportunity to binge and purge. Eventually, she became so overwhelmed by the disorder that she had to leave her teaching position and remain at home with her parents where she compulsively repeated this ritual throughout the day. The bulimia had progressed to a point where it controlled her life.

No one is born a bulimic. No one is ever born with a predisposition to bulimia that surfaces in later years. On the contrary, an individual may become a bulimic almost by chance. As we have seen, bulimics are usually individuals who have learned to turn to food in times of stress or as a means of finding a temporary escape from the severe anxiety they are experiencing. Such individuals also have a history of being extremely weight conscious, but because of their emotional reliance on food, they often have great difficulty remaining on a diet.

Initially, some bulimics may have heard of regurgitation as a means of purging and weight maintenance from a friend. Others may have read about it in a magazine or watched a program about bulimia or anorexia on television. Still others may have become disgusted with themselves for an excessive binge and come up with the idea on their own.

Some bulimics have said that they felt little guilt over their unusual secret rituals in the early stages of the disorder. In fact, the bulimic may at first feel proud that she has discovered a method which will allow her to binge without gaining weight. As her need to binge and vomit becomes increasingly intense with the passage of time, however, she will more likely come to feel that she has lost control over her life and eating habits.

The actual number of times a bulimic will binge and purge each day generally does not remain stable. Once an individual has turned to binging and purging as a means of coping with anxiety, her tendency to use this defense rapidly rises.

Eating and subsequent vomiting actually become integrated into the individual's life-style. This behavior turns into an accustomed response for those who need to eat for emotional reasons but cannot cope with the normal consequences of binge eating. In time the binge-purge syndrome may become the individual's way of handling any negative emotional experience, no matter how slight. Binging acts to blot out the disturbing feeling, and the purge serves to flush it out of the bulimic's system.

Eventually, if the condition remains untreated, the bulimic may feel compelled to binge and purge even when nothing unsettling has occurred in her life. This destructive behavior increases the sense of isolation and helplessness. Often bulimics, who usually present a cheerful exterior, are forced to deal with bouts of anger and depression. Even if the bulimic experiences feelings of desperation about her situation, without treatment she has few emotional resources to draw on. She will usually just wind up going on another binge followed by a purge, which simply reinforces her self-destructive addiction.

Mental health professionals are not sure why someone turns to bulimia in response to stress. They are certain, however, that it is an emotional disorder that becomes embedded in the individual's behavior as a result of specific mental conflicts. Individuals who might have become bulimic under a given set of circumstances are generally women with dependency problems. Most bulimics are psychologically dependent on the people around them.

Often these women do not appear to be overly dependent. On the contrary, many successfully camouflage these feelings by putting up a brave, resourceful, independent front in the professional or academic areas of their lives. Underneath it all, however, these women long to be taken care of by someone. It's almost as if they wish to be treasured little girls who will find unconditional love and support from the significant people in their lives. They want to relinquish responsibility for their own futures.

In conjunction with these wishes, however, the bulimic must cope with the anxiety-producing fear that the people on whom she wishes to depend will not allow her to do so. In effect, she continually places herself in a precarious position. She is afraid to express anger or assertive behavior for fear that the people she wants to care for her will not view any form of criticism or dissent from her as acceptable behavior. She fears that if she does not fulfill their expectations of her, they will ultimately reject her.

Often the doubts and anxieties expressed by bulimics have their origin in the girl's early childhood. Many mothers of bulimics have expressed concern over their own effectiveness as capable, dependable, functioning adults. These women frequently express doubts about their ability consistently to show tenderness and warmth. Such women often have difficulty perceiving themselves as adults capable of providing their child with a secure, healthful, loving environment for a sustained period of time. As a result of their own self-doubts, these mothers may react with tremendous anxiety when their child expresses the normal need for care and affection.

Their own feelings of insecurity about themselves may lead them to be less responsive than is desirable for the everyday needs and demands of a growing child. By interacting with their offspring in this manner, they are actually helping to create a sense of insecurity in the child. A little girl may come to feel that she is not "good" because she was scolded for wanting something, like her mother's attention, which she felt she genuinely needed. She'll come to believe she is not worthwhile because she has been disappointed when she asked for something that she felt deeply about.

The young child soon gathers from her mother's reaction that she had best become a capable, self-sufficient little person if she is to elicit any positive response at all from her parent. She has to learn to be independent and not to express her own needs, even if in actuality she longs to be nurtured and cared for.

The fathers of bulimics tend to avoid intimate involvement of any type with their daughters. Many of these men are quite successful in the business world. Like many fathers of anorectics, these men expect and demand an extremely high level of performance in all areas of their children's lives.

They tend to expect their daughters to be both beautiful and successful. The father of a bulimic generally does not want to know about weaknesses; he refuses to hear the words "I can't." He expects his daughter to strive for excellence and eventually to achieve it. The bulimic daughter may admire and respect her father and all he has accomplished, but she may feel extremely anxious about reaching the standards he has set for her.

Bulimic women turn to food as a response to fear and anxiety. They worry that they won't be able to meet successfully the high expectations of their parents as well as those of other significant people in their lives. They also tend to set for themselves unrealistically high aspirations, which they are continually anxious about attaining. These girls live with constant fear and insecurity.

One area of their existence that they do not perceive as threatening is that of food and eating. Turning to food may make them feel safe and secure if only for a short time. Food, unlike their parents, is something these girls can depend on. Eating is almost guaranteed to bring them a sense of pleasure.

Although binging initially may help to blot out their fears, the relief they experience is generally quite short-lived. Their fear of the weight gain that can result from a binge causes renewed anxiety. They may try to relieve this anxiety by purging, become caught up in a vicious cycle, and find that within a short period of time they have become full-fledged bulimics.

The Anorexia Nervosa Project at Michael Reese Medical Center in Chicago is primarily a research organization committed to investigating eating disorders. Over the last two years its staff members have interviewed numerous people, primarily women who are having difficulty with food or with their weight.

Recently, staff members have focused their efforts on the gorge-purge syndrome. Although their research is not yet complete, they have already learned a good deal about eating disorders:

"Most of the people seen in therapy, consultations, or interviews ate for a variety of emotional reasons. Often, over the years, they had chosen to eat rather than to experience a wide range of feelings such as anger, frustration, disappointment, loneliness, and boredom. Over time, food had become increasingly utilized to regulate these tensions and feelings, until it occupied a central role in that individual's life.

"If purging (through self-induced vomiting or the use of laxatives and enemas) is used to undo the gorging, then the gorging alternately becomes more uncontrollable. Once people realize that their body size no longer has to reflect the amount they eat, then eating often becomes more chaotic and unrestrained. What started out as a 'perfect solution' for eating and weight control quickly becomes a pernicious and destructive cycle that is difficult to relinquish."

Among the recommendations made by the project for victims of eating disorders are the following:

"Seek professional help." Most patients have experienced great difficulty making progress without some sort of therapy.

"If purging, find a competent internist and tell him or her the truth. Repeated vomiting and use of laxatives or diuretics can result in serious medical complications."

The medical consequences brought on by eating disorders can be severe. The following is a partial list of the physical problems that may be triggered by anorexia nervosa or bulimia:

Skin. Because of the reduced fluid intake as well as the excessive fluid elimination from the abuse of laxatives and diuretics, the individual's skin may become excessively dry. The victim may also suffer from dehydration. Frequent vomiting and laxative abuse may also cause a fine rash or pimples.

Salivary glands. Frequent vomiting causes the salivary glands to swell. The general area will become tender and somewhat painful. The individual will develop a sort of chipmunk face with swollen areas at the base of her chin.

Constipation. Constipation is a common problem of anorectics and bulimics because of their failure to take in or to retain sufficient food or fluid.

Edema (water retention). The edema that occurs in people with eating disorders is usually brought on by a combination of malnutrition, frequent vomiting, and the abuse of laxatives and diuretics. The victim suffers from an electrolyte imbalance due to the incorrect amounts of sodium and potassium in the system.

An electrolyte imbalance can cause muscle spasms, kidney problems, or cardiac arrest. When laxative or diuretic abuse is stopped, a difficult period follows during which bloating occurs until the body is able to respond again in a normal way. Some victims may have a similar experience while the body adjusts to a recent weight gain. In edema cases some swelling and puffiness generally occurs around the ankles and feet.

Bloating. A swelling in the stomach or abdomen often occurs as one of the results of prolonged starvation. Excessive vomiting and the abuse of laxatives or diuretics may also contribute to this problem. It is also partially the result of insufficient protein intake.

Abdominal pain, a feeling of fullness. These conditions may be partially caused by attitudes and emotions as well as by physical factors. Abdominal pain may result from hunger pangs, changes in the bowel, and an insufficient intake of food. A feeling of fullness may sometimes result from the fear involved with the intake of food, a fear that is common among victims of anorexia and bulimia.

Teeth. Inadequate nourishment, frequent vomiting, and a diet that is almost devoid of protein may result in numerous cavities and the erosion of tooth enamel. According to Stanley Flander, a New York City dentist, the acid environment that develops in the mouth as a result of continuous regurgitation will result in increased tooth decay as well.

Amenorrhea. A lack of body fat, rigorous athletic training, and emotional turbulence may result in the cessation of the individual's menstrual period. The body becomes unable to produce the hormones necessary for menstruation.

Hair loss and breakage. Many anorectics find their hair becoming dry and brittle. In some cases strands of hair may actually break or even fall out. This is a result of inadequate nutrition.

Anorexia nervosa and bulimia are dangerous eating disorders that have become widespread. They claim more than half a million victims in this country alone. There are thousands of new victims each year.

Some individuals suffer lifelong problems as the result of their affliction. Some even die. If left untreated, these illnesses can be highly destructive to the individual as well as to her family. Anorexia and bulimia can be treated, however, and that's what the next chapter is all about.

Chapter
8
HELP

ANAD (National Association for Anorexia Nervosa and Associated Disorders) in Highland Park, Illinois, was the first national nonprofit educational self-help organization in America dedicated to alleviating the eating disorders we have discussed.

ANAD came into existence in response to the needs of anorectics and their families. It offers a number of services free of charge. Among them are counseling, information, referrals, self-help groups for both victims and parents, educational programs, and a listing of therapists, hospitals, and clinics treating anorectics. The group also encourages research.

ANAD offers the following advice to individuals who think that they might be either anorectic or bulimic: "Learn as much as you can about anorexia nervosa, with emphasis on articles, etc., on bulimia. If you are keeping the problem a secret, try to understand that you can best overcome it by seeking help. Locate and go to a therapist (psychologist, medical doctor, social worker, etc.) who understands and treats anorexia and bulimia.

"Join a self-help group if there is one in your area. If none exists, form one if you feel capable of leading a group. Become a resource person responding to others by mail or telephone, or assist ANAD in bringing attention to this problem and participating in programs to educate the public and health professionals.

"Many anorectics have a low sense of self-esteem. This may be improved by learning to be more assertive. Assertiveness training courses are offered in various places. If courses are not available, read the books listed below. Many other titles on the subject are also available."

Alberti, Robert E., and Emmons, Michael L. *Your Perfect Right*. San Luis Obispo, Calif.: Impact, 1970–74.

Butler, Pamela E. *Self-Assertion for Women*. New York: Harper & Row, 1981.

Stanlee, Phelps, and Austin, Nancy. *The Assertive Woman*. San Luis Obispo, Calif.: Impact, 1975.

ANAD has also produced a list providing a brief description of some therapies used for anorexia nervosa and bulimia. They are as follows:

Family therapy. Treatment focuses on changing patterns of family interaction. The length of therapy is usually approximately six months with an 80 to 90 percent rate of cure.

Psychotherapy. When used in conjuction with eating disorders, treatment focuses on the problems of low self-esteem, guilt, anxiety, depression, and a sense of helplessness. Treatment time averages between two and three years.

Hypnosis. Some therapists employ this technique, but anorectics who fear a semblance of control by others may resist hypnosis. Some success has been claimed by therapists who teach self-hypnosis and biofeedback techniques to their patients during three to six months of hospitalization.

Brief therapy. A variety of techniques are employed to stop the gorging and vomiting while other methods assist in the achievement of independence. Treatment time is usually about three months.

ANAD's literature states, "It is apparent that therapy sometimes appears to be effective in a relatively short time even though the individual may have seen therapists previously. This may in part be due to the individual's readiness for change, an effective therapist, or a special empathy between therapist and patient.

"When recovery is achieved through short-term therapy, one must be aware that the return to a completely whole personality may require further explanation and support."

ANAD has the following suggestions for self-help. The organization warns, however, that these suggestions are not a substitute for psychological treatment.

"Relaxation techniques. General relaxation exercises, guided imagery, self-hypnosis, meditation, or any relaxation techniques you have used. Relaxation may help to reduce overactivity or relieve food-related anxieties. It may be used before or after eating to eliminate binges. When proficiency is gained, feelings of relaxation may be projected in a specific situation rather than just at a time of stress. It should be useful to both starvers and stuffers.

"Classes in techniques of relaxation are often available as recreational or self-improvement courses in colleges, high schools, or YMCAs. Instruction is advisable, but if necessary books can provide sufficient understanding to practice the skills.

"Overeaters Anonymous has proven very helpful to some who gorge and/or purge.

"Nutrition counselors have been very helpful to many bulimics and to some starvers. They provide information about healthful foods and reassurance that adequate calories can maintain both slimness and a healthy body. If you are unable to see a nutrition counselor, it may be helpful to know a rule of thumb for maintaining weight. The moderately active person requires fifteen calories per pound per day. For a desired weight of 110 pounds, use the formula $15 \times 110 = 1,650$ calories a day.

"If laxative abuse is a problem, here are a few suggestions that may be helpful. First, if one is eating or retaining very small quantities of food, there may be nothing to eliminate, bowel movements may be very infrequent, and the bowel may become distended with gas. Second, adequate intake and retention of liquid is very important in avoiding constipation. Drink six glasses of water, fruit juice, or milk daily. Third, the importance of bulk has been recently stressed by many doctors. If you want to eliminate the use of laxatives, but are afraid to go without anything at all, why not try using natural laxatives such as fresh fruits, vegetables, prunes, rhubarb, and bran? Bran may be purchased as shredded wheat or bran cereals. Use one to two ounces of bran each day. Reports suggest that bowel disturbances from these changes in eating habits are troublesome, but bearable, usually subsiding within a few weeks."

ANAD strongly recommends that individuals suffering from eating disorders find a therapist to help them with their problem. The organization has put together the following suggestions for finding a therapist and remaining in therapy:

"Since there are many philosophies concerning the treatment of anorexia nervosa and many personality differences in both patients and therapists, ANAD strongly recommends that you explore the suitability of the therapist from a very personal standpoint to ensure finding the therapist who can work best with you or with you and your family.

"The therapist's rapport with you (and your family, if this applies) and your approval of the treatment approach are important considerations.

"If the symptoms appear to you to indicate anorexia nervosa or bulimia but the therapist suggests that no problem exists or recommends that you handle the problem without treatment at this time, do not hesitate to seek another opinion.

"Nor should you hesitate to seek another therapist if, after a reasonable time, you can see no progress. Of course you should first discuss your feelings. You should make a decision after considering the points of discussion in light of your own feelings.

"If therapists' fees are too high, check local, state, or county mental health facilities or private welfare agencies that operate on a sliding scale. Any therapist who is willing to work with an anorectic on the problems of low self-esteem, depression, anxiety, and guilt should produce some positive results, providing a good therapeutic relationship has been established."

William N. Davis is the director of the Center for the Study of Anorexia, a division of the Institute for Contemporary Psychotherapy, in New York City. According to Dr. Davis, "In many instances, the anorectic who is brought into treatment will pretend that everything is okay, when in reality things are not that way at all." In a recent interview Dr. Davis went on to explain how both anorexia nervosa and bulimia can often be a response to stress, to loneliness, and to a more general dependency reflected in a feeling of "what am I going to do with the rest of my life now?"

According to Dr. Davis, "Anorectics believe their parents need to depend on them. The parents of anorectics need to sit down with each other and together create a policy for living constructively within their household, a policy they feel they can support and adhere to. They need to learn to separate from their daughter and at the same time come across as genuine parents. Mothers of anorectics tend to be too intrusive and overinvolved with their children. The parents of an anorectic cannot afford to continue to act helpless. They must assume a leadership role.''

The Center for the Study of Anorexia has four objectives: effective treatment, specialized training, significant research, and increased community understanding. In its pursuit of these objectives, the center is guided by the conviction that anorexia nervosa is primarily a psychological disorder, although secondary problems that are medical in nature can and do occur.

The Center for the Study of Anorexia is composed of five separate divisions:

Treatment. Treatment services include individual and family consultations and individual, conjoint, and family psychotherapy. Medical consultation or referral can be arranged as necessary. Individual consultants with psychotherapists who treat anorectics can be arranged on request.

Training. Available to selected mental health professionals, the training program provides instruction in the understanding and psychological treatment of anorexia.

New York Anorexia Aid. Intended to be an adjunct to psychotherapy but not restricted to those in treatment, NYAA conducts group meetings for anorectics and for parents or spouses of anorectics.

Prevention. Preventive services include lectures, seminars, and workshops for interested community groups, and programs designed to promote a higher level of awareness of anorexia among the general public.

Research. The research division designs and conducts both

clinical and empirical studies intended to increase knowledge of the demography, etiology (causes), and treatment of anorexia.

The Center for the Study of Anorexia is located at One West Ninety-first Street, New York, New York 10028. There are no geographic restrictions regarding applications for the center's services. For further information about the center and the services it provides, call (212) 595-3449. Calls are received by the center on a twenty-four-hour basis.

Center Director William Davis describes the process this way: "When a potential patient or a family member calls the center, someone trained to talk to such a person will answer the phone. An appointment for an initial consultation will probably be made. This consultation will usually be completed in one to three visits.

"After the consultation the patient will be assigned to one of the staff therapists. The patient may also be assigned to a support group for outside help." Dr. Davis added that the patients are required to have a medical examination.

Judith Brisman and Ellen Schor are co-directors of the Associates for Bulimia and Related Eating Disorders in New York City. According to Dr. Brisman, "Bulimics stuff their real feelings down with food—anger, vulnerability, loneliness, all of it. They fall into a habit which then becomes out of control. They have to learn to stop binging to enable themselves to get rid of the triggers that signal a purge. At the center, they'll learn to identify the red-light items that lead to a binge. Then they'll work on isolating alternatives to binging.

"Bulimia is spreading because people were allowed to be fat before. Now fashion dictates that they have to be thin. Even the word 'excess' has taken on a negative connotation. The problem can lead to very serious complications. Often the women who come to see us for help have a full set of dentures. Some suffer from ulcers. One woman swallowed a spoon while gagging herself in order to throw up. There have also been documented deaths from heart ruptures."

Dr. Schor added, "Bulimic women tend to be perfectionists. They are often pretty, well groomed, and afraid of losing control. It seems as if these women never really learned to set limits. They've either placed very strict restrictions on themselves or tried to live with no limits at all. They work for a guise of respectability and often don't show their real feelings at all."

Dr. Schor once suffered from bulimia herself. She described her feelings this way: "Sometimes I felt as if I were crazy. I had this terrible secret to guard of which I felt so ashamed. I was terrified of it, but at the same time it was my greatest ally. I had to learn to set realistic limits for myself. I felt under tremendous pressure to be perfect, and I found myself trying to meet impossible standards.

"One night while I was still bulimic, I had invited my mother to spend the night with me at my apartment. When she saw me gorging, she asked me why I was eating so ravenously, pausing to mention that I had enjoyed an ample dinner earlier that evening.

"I indicated to her that everything was all right. I was not going to become fat from this food, as I intended to throw it all up momentarily. My mother was horrified. She told me that she refused to remain in my home if I continued this behavior. I had eaten a great deal. I felt I had to purge, so I was forced to let my mother leave. It was then that I realized that I had to get help."

Ellen Schor eventually did get help. She is no longer a bulimic and now operates the center to help other victims of eating disorders rid themselves of their affliction. The

Associates for Bulimia and Related Eating Disorders offers the Bulimia Workshop: A Program for the Treatment of Binge-Purge Eating Disorders. It is described as follows:

Treatment Philosophy and Purpose of the Bulimia Workshop

The purpose of the Bulimia Workshop is to educate clients about bulimia and help them take control over eating patterns which they believe are out of their control.

We do not believe that it is possible to induce long-term effects from one weekend or one month of treatment. However, our philosophy of treatment is based on the rationale that direct and immediate intervention into the binge-purge behavior is necessary. The bulimic's denial of the severity of this problem must be confronted and the binge-purge cycle must be interrupted before the bulimic can start on the road to longer term care for the problem. We will therefore approach the eating disorder directly through education, behavioral intervention, exploration of emotional denial, and extensive follow-up planning.

Treatment procedures will involve: 1) confrontation of the perfectionist facade of the bulimic and 2) development of alternatives to the binge-purge cycle that will in fact be nurturing, supportive, and ego-building.

The Bulimia Workshop will be held in New York City for a full weekend, with post-workshop sessions (described below).

Clients will be screened by telephone, questionnaire, and medical evaluations. If clinical or diagnostic questions arise, personal interviews by group leaders will be required. Screening procedures will attempt to eliminate persons in need of medical care and/or more intensive and immediate psychiatric care. Also persons who have eating disorders other than bulimia will not be accepted into treatment. All persons not accepted will be referred to other sources for evaluation, treatment, or support.

The Bulimia Workshop will receive phone calls requesting treatment or information about treatment on a twenty-four-hour basis. A telephone service will be used to take messages when secretarial personnel are not available.

Workshop Treatment Procedures

The first evening of treatment (Friday, 1:00–10:00) will be devoted to educating clients about the physiological and psychological aspects of bulimia. A one-hour lecture during this time will describe the physiological aspects of this disorder. The perfectionist and victim roles associated with binge-purging will be identified and confronted as psychological factors. The relationship between emotions and binging-purging will also be explored.

The second day (Saturday, 9:00–6:00) will consist of a functional analysis of the eating disorder for each participant. Situational and internal cues evoking the binge-purge pattern will be explored. Alternative coping skills for both the binge and the purge will be established. Both the lunch and the evenings following the workshop will be integrated into the program as a means of exploring "in vivo" [in life] examples of the attitudes and feelings associated with eating.

Throughout the weekend, assertiveness skills will be taught and role-played as alternatives to victimlike patterns.

Other behavioral techniques to be incorporated into the weekend are as follows: 1) cognitive restructuring [new ways of thinking], 2) development of delay procedures to postpone the reinforcing purge, and 3) self-monitoring skills and techniques to assess progress so as to maintain changes. The establishment of contracts with other participants to monitor and change the binging and purging will be an important aspect of follow-up to this workshop.

During the last day of the workshop (Sunday, 9:00–12:00) the work of the previous two days will be reinforced. Relaxation techniques will also be introduced as an alternative means of coping with stress. Follow-up social networks will be developed and binge-control contracts will be planned.

Follow-up Treatment

Follow-up to the workshop program is an essential, critical part of treatment. Follow-up will take two directions: 1) Support networks will be established during the workshop and reinforced as a part of post-workshop treatment. Ongoing communication with group leaders and other bulimics will be formally planned.

During the workshop, clients will be urged to establish support networks with other workshop participants. This will consist of developing a buddy system to provide telephone support, to monitor contracts (see below), and to urge clients to turn toward people, not food, for support. This system will also minimize the feelings of loneliness, hopelessness, and isolation that may cause binging.

As part of the program, clients will develop contracts establishing reinforcement contingencies for stopping the binge and purge. Alternatives to the eating disorder will be established, and means of monitoring one's behavior will be decided. The contracts will be shared with other clients (in particular, with buddies), and ways of communicating after the workshop and supporting each other in maintaining the contracts will be developed.

A three-hour follow-up session will be scheduled one

week following the workshop weekend. Subsequently, optional two hour post-workshop sessions will be held with group leaders present at all sessions. Post-workshop treatment will be aimed at monitoring and reinforcing behavior change, exploring feelings associated with these changes, and easing clients into more extensive, longer-term treatment or self-help groups, as needed. In addition, information regarding nutrition and health care will be provided (at the two hour sessions) by persons with expertise in these areas.

Three-, six-, and twelve-month follow-up calls to clients will provide continued support measures as well as opportunities to establish treatment outcome data for research purposes.

Recovering bulimics will be encouraged to attend the one-hour post-workshop sessions, which will continue throughout the year following each weekend workshop. They will be encouraged both to contribute positive experiences that have led to behavior change and to make use of a continuing and growing support network.

2) The necessity of long-term treatment in addition to our workshop will be stressed. Clients will be provided with referrals ranging from self-help groups (WW [Weight Watchers], binge-purge self-help networks, etc.) to more formal types of psychotherapy. Clients will be clinically assessed on an individual basis to determine appropriate referral sources. As a part of this system, we will have available the names of programs and nutritional experts for aid in the development of healthful eating patterns.

There are many varied approaches to the treatment of eating disorders. In all of them, however, the therapist must eventually integrate a psychological or behavioral approach with medical and nutritional expertise. Solving family problems at home and establishing a trusting relationship between patient and therapist is also of extreme importance. It is essential that the focus of the therapy is not only on restoring the patient to a normal weight but also on working on the underlying troublesome problems.

In some way the patient must be convinced that she has a right as well as an obligation to herself to live her life in a way that is uniquely her own. Only with this recognition and the commitment to work toward developing a new assertive sense of self will these often beautiful and talented young women learn how to stop starving themselves.

BIBLIOGRAPHY

Brenner, M. "Bulimarexia." *Savvy*, June 1980.

Brody, Jane. "An Eating Disorder of Binges and Purges." *The New York Times,* October 20, 1981.

Chernin, Kim. *The Obsession.* New York: Harper & Row, 1981.

Frumkes, Lewis. "The Neurotic Personality." *Harper's Bazaar,* March 1982.

Levenkron, Steven. *The Best Little Girl in the World.* New York: Warner Books, 1979.

Liu, Aimee. *Solitaire.* New York: Harper & Row, 1979.

Millman, Marcia. *Such a Pretty Face.* New York: Norton, 1980.

Orbach, S. *Fat Is a Feminist Issue.* New York: Paddington Press, 1978.

Squire, Susan. "Why Thousands of Women Don't Know How to Eat Normally Anymore." *Glamour,* October 1981.

Weber, Melva. "Slim Overeaters' Disease." *Vogue,* October 1980.

Young, Nancy. "Full Stomachs, Empty Lives." *Glamour,* September 1979.

INDEX